What's for dinner?

It's a question busy families face every night of the week. And it's not always such an easy one to answer!

Welcome to **McCormick® 3-Step Cooking with Flavor.** We think this collection of more than 100 new recipes will make it a whole lot easier to prepare flavorful homemade meals any night of the week.

We've packed this book with delicious and nutritious main-dish recipes that will satisfy your family's appetite. We've also included some side-dish options, breakfast recipes, and, of course, a selection of sweet treats for when you have a few minutes to spare. And because the book is organized by main ingredient, you can thumb directly to the section you need—whether you have a package of ground beef in the fridge or a box of pasta in the pantry.

Each recipe has at least two Flavor Variations, so you can really enjoy each one at least three ways—more than 300 recipes, all with three steps or less. That's nearly a year's worth of dinners!

For more than 100 years, McCormick has been inspired by flavor and we want to share that passion with you. But the options don't end with the last page of this cookbook! Visit mccormick.com for even more ways to enjoy flavor.

Happy cooking!

The McCormick Test Kitchens

Publisher Richard Fraiman
General Manager Steven Sandonato
Executive Director, Marketing Services Carol Pittard
Director, Retail & Special Sales Tom Mifsud
Director, New Product Development Peter Harper
Assistant Director, Brand Marketing Laura Adam
Associate Counsel Helen Wan
Marketing Manager Victoria Alfonso
Senior Brand Manager, TWRS/M Holly Oakes
Design & Prepress Manager Anne-Michelle Gallero
Book Production Manager Susan Chodakiewicz

Special thanks Alexandra Bliss, Glenn Buonocore, Margaret Hess, Suzanne Janso, Dennis Marcel, Robert Marasco, Brooke Reger, Mary Sarro-Waite, Ilene Schreider, Adriana Tierno, Alex Voznesenskiy

Published by Time Inc. Home Entertainment

Time Inc.
1271 Avenue of the Americas
New York, New York 10020

ISBN 10: 1-60320-025-8
ISBN 13: 978-1-60320-025-7
Library of Congress Control Number: 2008903244

PRINTED IN CHINA

We welcome your comments and suggestions.
Please write to us at:
McCormick 3-Step Cooking with Flavor
Attention: Book Editors
PO Box 11016
Des Moines, IA 50336-1016

If you would like to order any of our hardcover Collector's Edition books, please call us at 1-800-327-6388. (Monday through Friday, 7:00 a.m.— 8:00 p.m. or Saturday, 7:00 a.m.—6:00 p.m. Central Time).

McCormick Inc. US Consumer Product Division
Senior Product Manager Céline Endler

Copyright 2008 McCormick & Company, Inc.

Special thanks to: Margaret Kime for her generous support and inspiration; Michael Pohuski for his vision; Colleen McIntosh for her unique sense of style; Robin Lutz Weiner for her flexibility and talent for making every dish looking extraordinary; Katrina Tekavec for her ability to make food look beautiful, yet so simple; Alan Bird for his magical touch-ups.

This book would not have come together without you. Thanks!

Food Photography Michael Pohuski
Food Stylists Robin Lutz Weiner and Katrina Tekavec
Prop Stylist Colleen McIntosh

Spices, Herbs & Extracts Photography Mark Thomas

President Julie Merberg
Editor Sara Newberry
Design Elizabeth van Itallie
Recipe Consultant Judith Choate

Special thanks Sarah Parvis, Patty Brown, Pam Abrams, Kate Gibson

3-STEP
Cooking with
FLAVOR

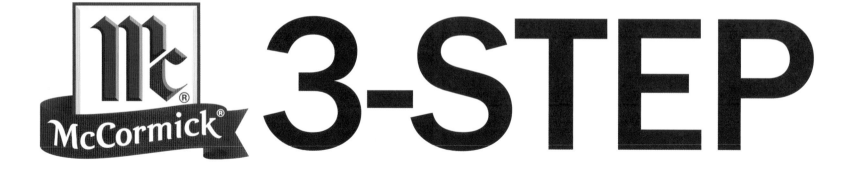

3-STEP

Cooking with
FLAVOR

Contents

Pantry Staples

One of the easiest ways to make dinnertime less stressful is have a fully-stocked pantry, refrigerator and freezer. Over the next few pages we have listed products that are useful to keep on hand for everyday meals.

IN THE REFRIGERATOR

Along with the usual suspects (milk, eggs, butter), it's not a bad idea to keep a few different kinds of cheese in the fridge. Sour cream and yogurt are also handy to add richness and flavor to soups and sauces.

Dairy
Eggs
Butter
Milk
Cream
Half-and-half
Sour cream
Plain yogurt
Ricotta cheese
Cream cheese
Feta cheese crumbles
Grated Parmesan cheese
Shredded Mozzarella cheese
Shredded Mexican blend cheese
Shredded Cheddar cheese
Shredded Monterey Jack cheese
Sliced Provolone cheese
Sliced Swiss cheese

IN THE FREEZER

Frozen fruits and vegetables are great staples—picked at the peak of freshness and quick-frozen, they often have more nutritional value than their fresh counterparts do by the time they make it to your supermarket's produce department. Keep bread, nuts and value packs of meat and poultry in the freezer also and use them as you need them.

Vegetables & Fruits
Artichokes
Bell pepper stir-fry (with onion)
Broccoli
Carrots
Corn
Green beans
Chopped onion
Spinach
Summer squash
Winter squash
Blueberries
Peaches
Strawberries

Nuts & Fruits
Slivered almonds
Peanuts
Pecans
Walnuts

Bread
French bread
Hamburger buns
Hard rolls
Prepared pie crusts
Prepared pizza crusts
Sub rolls
Tortillas

Meat & Poultry
Bacon
Sliced turkey pepperoni
Sausage (pre-cooked and raw)

IN THE PANTRY

A well-stocked pantry is a home cook's best friend. From baking essentials to spices and seasonings, this can serve as "command central" in the kitchen.

Mixes & Baking Needs

Stuffing mix
Kosher salt
Granulated sugar
Powdered sugar
Brown sugar
All-purpose flour

Pasta, Grains & Bread

Couscous
Pasta (different shapes)
Egg noodles
White rice
Brown rice
Pearl barley
Polenta
Plain breadcrumbs
Panko (Japanese breadcrumbs)
Croutons
Tortilla chips
Tostadas
Taco shells

Oils, Vinegars & Wines

Nonstick cooking spray
Olive oil
Sesame oil
Vegetable oil
Balsamic vinegar
Cider vinegar
Red wine vinegar
White wine vinegar
Dry red wine
Dry white wine
Marsala wine

Broths, Sauces & Condiments

(refrigerate after opening)
Beef broth
Chicken broth
Vegetable broth
Barbecue sauce
Blue cheese dressing
Honey
Hot pepper sauce
Pure maple syrup
Molasses
Soy sauce
Worcestershire sauce
Dijon mustard
Ketchup
Mayonnaise
Peanut butter
Salsa

Canned Fruits & Vegetables

(refrigerate after opening)
Artichoke hearts
Whole beans
Refried beans
Baby corn
Fruit preserves & jams
Chopped green chiles
Olives
Pineapple chunks
Roasted red peppers
Crushed tomatoes
Diced tomatoes
Tomato paste
Tomato sauce
Water chestnuts

THE SPICE SHELF

Sometimes a splash of this or a dash of that will take a meal to the next level. Here is a list of the products that will help you do just that! (see page 11 for tips on keeping dried herbs, spices and seasonings fresh).

Extracts

Almond Extract
Lemon Extract
Orange Extract
Peppermint Extract
Pure Vanilla Extract
Rum Extract

Seasoning Blends & Mixes

Beef Stew Seasoning
Chili Seasoning
Hamburger Seasoning
Lemon Pepper
Meatloaf Seasoning
Grill Mates® Mesquite Seasoning
Grill Mates® Montreal Chicken
    Seasoning
Grill Mates® Montreal Spicy Steak
    Seasoning
Grill Mates® Montreal Steak
    Seasoning
Grill Mates® Low-Sodium Montreal
    Steak Seasoning
Chili Seasoning Mix
Taco Seasoning Mix
Sloppy Joe Seasoning
Slow Cookers BBQ Pulled Pork
    Seasoning

Slow Cookers Italian Herb
  Chicken Seasoning
Pot Roast Seasoning Mix
Poultry Seasoning Mix
Salad Supreme® Seasoning

Spices, Herbs & Seasonings
Ground Allspice
Apple Pie Spice
Basil Leaves
Bay Leaf
Black Peppercorn Grinder
Coarse Ground Black Pepper
Ground Black Pepper
Celery Salt
Celery Seed
Chili Powder
Chives
Cinnamon Sugar
Whole Cloves
Dill Weed
Ground Sage

Ground Thyme
Italian Seasoning
Ground Cinnamon
Cinnamon Stick
Cinnamon Sugar
Ground Cloves
Curry Powder
Ground Cumin
Garlic Pepper
Garlic Powder
Garlic Salt
California Style® Wet Garlic
Ground Ginger
Ground Mustard
Mustard Seed
Ground Nutmeg
OLD BAY® Seasoning
Minced Onion
Onion Powder
Onion Salt
Oregano Leaves
Paprika

Parsley Flakes
Pepper Medley Grinder
Pumpkin Pie Spice
Crushed Red Pepper
Ground Red Pepper
Rosemary Leaves
Rubbed Sage Leaves
Seasoned Salt
Sesame Seed
Ground Turmeric
Thyme Leaves

Gravy & Sauce Mixes
Au Jus Gravy Mix
Brown Gravy Mix
Low-Sodium Brown Gravy Mix
Chicken Gravy Mix
Country Gravy Mix
Enchilada Sauce Mix
Onion Gravy
Pork Gravy Mix
Turkey Gravy Mix

Conversion Table for Cooking

● **VOLUME**

1 teaspoon = 5 mL
1 tablespoon = 15 mL
1 fluid ounce = 30 mL
1 cup = 240 mL
2 cups (1 pint) = 470 mL
4 cups (1 quart) = 0.95 liter
4 quarts (1 gallon) = 3.8 liters

● **WEIGHT**

1 ounce = 28 grams
1 pound = 454 grams

● **AREA**
¼ inch = 6 mm
½ inch = 1 cm
1 inch = 3 cm

● **TEMPERATURE**

°F	°C
225	110
250	120
275	135
300	150
325	160
350	180
375	190
400	205
425	220
450	230
475	245
500	260

Keeping Dried Herbs and Spices Fresh

For the most flavor, keep your spices only as long as their flavor lasts.

Ground spices	2 to 3 years
Whole spices	3 to 4 years
Seasoning blends	1 to 2 years
Herbs	1 to 3 years
Extracts*	4 years

Here are some tips for keeping your spices fresh as long as possible (and for finding out if it is time to replace them):

- Check the color of your spices and herbs. If it has faded, chances are the flavor has too.

- Rub or crush the spice or herb in your hand. If the aroma is weak, it's time to replace it.

- Store herbs and spices in tightly capped containers and keep them away from heat, moisture and direct sunlight.

- To minimize moisture and caking, use a dry measuring spoon and avoid sprinkling directly from the jar into a steaming pot. Replace lids immediately after use and make sure they are tightly closed.

- Check the freshness date on the bottom or right side of the bottle to help keep track of when it's time to toss (visit www.mccormick.com for more information).

* (except Pure Vanilla Extract, which lasts indefinitely)

Chicken & Turkey

Grilled Chili-Lime Chicken

PREP TIME: 15 minutes · MARINATE TIME: 30 minutes · COOK TIME: 8 minutes

Juice and zest of 2 limes
2 tablespoons olive or canola oil
2 tablespoons **Chili Powder**
1 tablespoon honey
¼ teaspoon salt
¼ teaspoon **Ground Red Pepper,** optional
6 boneless, skinless chicken breasts,
   (1½ pounds)

Mango Salsa (see page 59), for serving,
   optional

1 **MIX** lime juice, oil, Chili Powder, honey, salt and Ground Red Pepper, if using, in a resealable plastic bag. Add the chicken, seal and knead to coat. Refrigerate 30 minutes. Remove chicken from bag, discard marinade.

2 **GRILL** over medium-high heat, turning frequently, 8 minutes or until chicken is cooked through. Serve with Mango Salsa, if desired.

► **MAKES 6 SERVINGS**

flavor variations

● MONTREAL GRILLED CHICKEN
Substitute 2 tablespoons **Grill Mates®
Montreal Chicken Seasoning** for Chili Powder and Ground Red Pepper. Prepare as directed.

● GRILLED CHICKEN
Substitute 2 tablespoons **Seasoned Salt** for Chili Powder and Ground Red Pepper. Prepare as directed.

Grilled Citrus-Glazed Chicken

PREP TIME: 5 minutes · MARINATE TIME: 5 minutes · COOK TIME: 12 minutes

1½ cup frozen orange juice concentrate,
    thawed
2 tablespoons honey
1 tablespoon low-sodium soy sauce
½ teaspoon **Garlic Salt**
1 teaspoon **Lemon Pepper**
½ teaspoon **Mustard Seed**
4 boneless, skinless chicken breast halves
    (1 pound)

1 **COMBINE** orange juice concentrate, honey, soy sauce, Garlic Salt, Lemon Pepper and Mustard Seed in a resealable plastic bag. Add chicken, seal and press to coat. Remove chicken from bag, discard marinade.

2 **GRILL** over medium-high heat, turning frequently, 12 minutes or until nicely glazed and cooked through.

▶ **MAKES 4 SERVINGS**

flavor variations

● **GRILLED CHILI-CITRUS CHICKEN**
Substitute 1 teaspoon **Chili Powder** for Garlic Salt. Prepare as directed.

● **GRILLED CURRY-CITRUS CHICKEN**
Add 1 teaspoon **Curry Powder** to glaze mixture. Prepare as directed.

● **GRILLED ONIONY CITRUS CHICKEN**
Substitute ½ teaspoon **Onion Salt** for Garlic Salt. Prepare as directed.

Grilled Herb-Mustard Chicken

PREP TIME: 10 minutes · MARINATE TIME: 30 minutes · COOK TIME: 8 minutes

½ cup vegetable oil
¼ cup Dijon mustard
2 tablespoons **Italian Seasoning**
½ teaspoon **Basil Leaves**
½ teaspoon **Oregano Leaves**
½ teaspoon **Garlic Powder**
½ teaspoon salt
4 boneless, skinless chicken breasts
  (1 pound)

1 STIR together oil, mustard, Italian Seasoning, Basil Leaves, Oregano Leaves, Garlic Powder and salt in a resealable plastic bag. Add chicken and toss to coat well. Refrigerate 30 minutes. Remove chicken from marinade. Discard any remaining marinade.

2 GRILL over medium-high heat, turning frequently, 8 minutes or until chicken is cooked through.

► MAKES 4 SERVINGS

flavor variations

● **GRILLED PROVENÇAL CHICKEN**
Substitute ½ teaspoon **Marjoram Leaves,** 1 teaspoon **Thyme Leaves,** 1 teaspoon **Basil Leaves,** 1 teaspoon **Rosemary Leaves,** ½ teaspoon **Rubbed Sage** and ½ teaspoon **Fennel Seed** for Italian Seasoning, Basil Leaves, Oregano Leaves and Garlic Powder. Prepare as directed.

● **GRILLED TARRAGON CHICKEN**
Substitute 2 tablespoons **Tarragon Leaves** for Italian Seasoning. Omit Oregano Leaves and Basil Leaves. Prepare as directed.

● **GRILLED HERB-MUSTARD VEGETABLES**
Marinate red and yellow bell peppers, whole green onions, red onion wedges and mushrooms with chicken. Add to grill 10 minutes before chicken is cooked.

Grilled Lemon-Rosemary Chicken

PREP TIME: 5 minutes · MARINATE TIME: 30 minutes · COOK TIME: 12 minutes

½ cup olive oil
1 tablespoon lemon juice
1 tablespoon **Grill Mates® Montreal Chicken Seasoning**
1 teaspoon **Rosemary Leaves**
¼ teaspoon **California Style® Wet Garlic**
4 boneless, skinless chicken breast halves (1 pound)

1 **COMBINE** olive oil, lemon juice, Chicken Seasoning, Rosemary Leaves and Wet Garlic in resealable plastic bag. Add chicken, seal, and press to coat evenly. Refrigerate 30 minutes. Remove chicken from bag, brushing off any excess marinade; discard marinade.

2 **GRILL** 12 minutes, turning frequently, or until chicken is cooked through.

► MAKES 4 SERVINGS

flavor variations

● GRILLED ITALIAN
   LEMON-ROSEMARY CHICKEN
Substitute **Italian Seasoning** for Chicken Seasoning. Add ¼ teaspoon <u>each</u> salt <u>and</u> **Ground Black Pepper.** Prepare as directed.

● GRILLED MESQUITE
   LEMON-ROSEMARY CHICKEN
Substitute 1 tablespoon **Grill Mates®** **Mesquite Seasoning** for Chicken Seasoning. Prepare as directed.

Sesame Chicken

PREP TIME: 15 minutes · COOK TIME: 15 minutes

2 tablespoons flour
2 tablespoons fine breadcrumbs
¼ cup (1 ounce) **Sesame Seed**
2 teaspoons **Parsley Flakes**
1 teaspoon **Onion Salt**
½ teaspoon **Ground Ginger**
¼ teaspoon **Ground Black Pepper**
4 boneless, skinless chicken breast halves
　(1 pound)
2　tablespoons vegetable oil

1 **MIX** flour, breadcrumbs, Sesame Seed, Parsley Flakes, Onion Salt, Ground Ginger and Ground Black Pepper in large shallow bowl. Coat both sides of chicken with mixture. Spray both sides of chicken with nonstick cooking spray. Place chicken in single layer on rimmed baking sheet.

2 **BAKE** in preheated 375°F oven 15 minutes or until chicken is cooked through.

► **MAKES 4 SERVINGS**

flavor variations

● SESAME-GARLIC CHICKEN
Substitute ¾ teaspoon **Garlic Salt** for Onion Salt. Prepare as directed.

● SESAME TURKEY
Use 6 turkey cutlets in place of chicken. Prepare as directed.

● SESAME-ORANGE SPINACH SALAD
Stir together 1 tablespoon sesame oil and 2 tablespoons vegetable oil. Whisk in 1 tablespoon lemon juice. Toss dressing with 3 cups washed baby spinach and 1 can mandarin orange segments, drained. Sprinkle with 1 tablespoon **Sesame Seed.** Serve with chicken.

Portobello-Tarragon Chicken

PREP TIME: 10 minutes · COOK TIME: 20 minutes

1 cup flour
1 teaspoon **Tarragon Leaves**
½ teaspoon salt
½ teaspoon **Ground Black Pepper**
6 boneless, skinless chicken breasts,
  (1½ pounds)
3 tablespoons olive <u>or</u> canola oil
1 teaspoon **California Style® Minced
  Wet Garlic**
6 ounces Portobello mushroom caps, sliced
1 teaspoon **Paprika**
¾ cup low-sodium chicken broth
1 cup sour cream

Cooked egg noodles, for serving (optional)

1 **MIX** flour, Tarragon Leaves, salt and Ground Black Pepper in shallow bowl. Coat chicken with mixture and set aside.

2 **HEAT** oil in large nonstick skillet over medium-high heat until very hot. Add chicken and cook 8 minutes, turning once, until golden. Remove chicken from skillet and keep warm.

3 **ADD** Wet Garlic and mushrooms to pan. Sprinkle with Paprika. Cook 5 minutes. Stir in broth and bring to a boil, stirring to scrape up any brown bits on bottom of pan. Cook 5 minutes or until liquid has reduced by half. Remove from heat and stir in sour cream. Spoon sauce over chicken and serve over egg noodles, if desired.

► **MAKES 6 SERVINGS**

flavor variations

● **WILD MUSHROOM–TARRAGON CHICKEN**
Use 1 cup mixed sliced wild mushrooms in place of the Portobello mushrooms. Prepare as directed.

● **PORTOBELLO-THYME CHICKEN**
Substitute 1 teaspoon **Thyme Leaves** for Tarragon Leaves. Prepare as directed.

Chicken Marsala

PREP TIME: 15 minutes · COOK TIME: 15 minutes

⅓ cup flour
½ teaspoon salt
1 teaspoon **Lemon Pepper**
6 boneless thinly sliced chicken breasts
  (1½ pounds)
2 tablespoons olive oil
3 tablespoons butter, divided
1 cup sliced Baby Bella mushrooms
½ teaspoon **Oregano Leaves**
¾ cup marsala or slightly sweet white wine
1 tablespoon lemon juice
1 tablespoon **Parsley Flakes**

1 **MIX** flour, salt and Lemon Pepper on large plate. Lightly coat chicken with mixture.

2 **HEAT** olive oil with 2 tablespoons of the butter in large nonstick skillet on medium-high heat. Add 3 pieces of chicken. Cook about 5 minutes, turning once, or until lightly colored. Remove chicken from skillet; keep warm. Repeat with remaining chicken.

3 **ADD** mushrooms and Oregano Leaves to skillet; cook until mushrooms are softened. Stir in wine and lemon juice to pan. Bring to boil, scraping up brown bits from bottom of pan. Stir in the remaining 1 tablespoon butter and cook for 2 minutes. Add Parsley Flakes and remove from heat. Spoon sauce over chicken and serve.

► **MAKES 6 SERVINGS**

flavor variations

● **LEMON CHICKEN WITH MUSHROOMS**
Use ¾ cup low-sodium chicken broth in place of Marsala. Prepare as directed.

● **LEMON-THYME CHICKEN**
Substitute 2 teaspoons **Thyme Leaves** for Parsley Flakes. Use low-sodium chicken broth and 1 additional tablespoon lemon juice in place of Marsala. Prepare as directed.

● **TURKEY MARSALA**
Use 6 boneless thinly sliced turkey breasts (1½ pounds) in place of chicken. Prepare as directed.

Salsa Chicken

PREP TIME: 5 minutes · COOK TIME: 15 minutes

1 package **Taco Seasoning Mix**
1 pound chicken tenders
2 tablespoons oil
1 can (14½ ounces) no salt added diced
   tomatoes, undrained
⅓ cup apricot or peach preserves

1 **PLACE** Taco Seasoning Mix in resealable plastic bag. Add chicken tenders; toss to coat.

2 **HEAT** oil in large skillet on medium heat. Add chicken; cook and stir 5 minutes or until chicken is lightly browned.

3 **STIR** in tomatoes and preserves. Reduce heat to low; cover and simmer 10 minutes until sauce is hot and chicken is cooked through.

► **MAKES 4 SERVINGS**

flavor variations

● **SALSA CHICKEN BREASTS**
Use 1 pound boneless, skinless chicken breast halves, cut in strips, in place of the chicken tenders. Prepare as directed.

● **RICE WITH CORN AND BLACK BEANS**
Cook rice according to package directions. Stir in 1 can corn, drained, and 1 can black beans, rinsed and drained.

● **MONTREAL SALSA CHICKEN**
Substitute 1½ teaspoons **Grill Mates® Montreal Chicken Seasoning** for the Taco Seasoning Mix. Prepare as directed.

Chicken Packets with Sun-dried Tomatoes and Olives

PREP TIME: 15 minutes · COOK TIME: 25 minutes

6 boneless, skinless chicken breasts
  (1½ pounds)
1 teaspoon **Basil Leaves**
1 teaspoon **Thyme Leaves**
½ teaspoon **Rosemary Leaves**
18 pieces sun-dried tomatoes packed in oil,
  well-drained, halved
½ cup sliced black olives
2 tablespoons olive oil
½ teaspoon salt
½ teaspoon **Ground Black Pepper**

1 **TEAR** 6 pieces aluminum foil large enough to completely enclose a chicken breast (12 to 14 inches long).

2 **PLACE** 1 chicken breast in center of each piece of foil. Mix Basil Leaves, Thyme Leaves and Rosemary Leaves and sprinkle each piece of chicken with ½ teaspoon mixture. Place 3 pieces of sun-dried tomato and a few olive slices on each piece of chicken. Drizzle each with 1 teaspoon olive oil and season with salt and Ground Black Pepper. Fold foil around chicken to seal and completely enclose chicken. Place packets in single layer on baking sheet.

3 **BAKE** in preheated 350°F oven 20 minutes or until chicken is cooked through. Serve individual packets to be opened at the table.

► **MAKES 6 SERVINGS**

. . . .

flavor variations

. . . .

● ITALIAN CHICKEN PACKETS
Substitute 1 tablespoon **Italian Seasoning** for Basil Leaves, Thyme Leaves and Rosemary Leaves. Drizzle chicken with Italian salad dressing in place of olive oil. Prepare as directed.

● CHICKEN PACKETS WITH PLUM
  TOMATOES AND OLIVES
Use 4 plum tomatoes cut into 3 slices each in place of sun-dried tomatoes. Prepare as directed.

● ROASTED BRUSSELS SPROUTS
These pair well with the chicken and cook in the same amount of time. Toss 3 cups frozen Brussels sprouts with 2 tablespoons olive oil and 1 teaspoon **Garlic Salt.** Spread in a single layer on baking sheet and bake at 350°F 20 minutes.

Herbed Chicken Fingers

PREP TIME: 15 minutes · COOK TIME: 12 minutes

½ cup panko (Japanese breadcrumbs)
½ cup plain breadcrumbs
1 teaspoon **Garlic Powder**
1 teaspoon **Dill Weed**
1 teaspoon **Parsley Flakes**
½ teaspoon salt
¼ teaspoon **Ground Black Pepper**
½ cup nonfat yogurt
½ teaspoon **Ground Mustard**
2 tablespoons water
1½ pounds chicken tenders

1 **MIX** panko, breadcrumbs, Garlic Powder, Dill Weed, salt and Ground Black Pepper in shallow bowl. Stir together yogurt, Ground Mustard and water in a second shallow bowl. Moisten chicken lightly with yogurt then roll in breadcrumb mixture. Place in a single layer on a nonstick rimmed baking sheet. Spray with nonstick spray.

2 **BAKE** in preheated 400°F oven 10 to 12 minutes or until coating is golden brown and chicken is cooked through. Serve with dipping sauces.

► **MAKES 6 SERVINGS**

flavor variations

● **MUSTARD DIPPING SAUCE**
Whisk ½ cup mayonnaise, 1 teaspoon **Ground Mustard,** ¼ cup honey and 2 tablespoons orange juice in small bowl until combined. Cover and refrigerate until ready to serve.

● **RANCH DIPPING SAUCE**
Stir ¾ cup buttermilk, ½ cup mayonnaise, 1 tablespoon **Parsley Flakes,** ½ teaspoon **Garlic Powder,** ¼ teaspoon salt and ⅛ teaspoon **Ground Red Pepper** in small bowl until smooth. Cover and refrigerate until ready to serve.

● **APRICOT DIPPING SAUCE**
Heat 1 cup apricot, peach or plum preserves, 1 tablespoon white vinegar, 2 tablespoons orange juice, 1 teaspoon **Ground Mustard,** ½ teaspoon **Minced Onion** and ¼ teaspoon **Ground Ginger** in small saucepan over low heat, stirring until preserves are melted and mustard and ginger have dissolved. Let cool slightly before serving.

Simple Chicken Curry with Pineapple Chutney

PREP TIME: 15 minutes · COOK TIME: 20 minutes

1 tablespoon peanut oil
1½ pounds skinless, boneless chicken, cut
    into 1-inch pieces
¾ teaspoon salt
¼ teaspoon **Ground Red Pepper,** optional
1 medium onion, minced
1 teaspoon **Garlic Powder**
1 teaspoon **Curry Powder**
½ cup low-sodium chicken broth
½ cup lite unsweetened coconut milk

Pineapple Chutney (recipe follows), optional
Cooked rice, for serving, optional

1 **HEAT** oil in a nonstick skillet over medium heat. Season chicken with salt and Ground Red Pepper. Add to pan and cook 4 minutes or just until chicken begins to color. Remove chicken from pan and keep warm.

2 **ADD** onion, Garlic Powder and Curry Powder to pan. Cook 3 minutes or until onion has softened. Return chicken to pan. Stir in broth and coconut milk. Simmer for 12 minutes or until chicken is cooked through and sauce has thickened. Serve with Pineapple Chutney and cooked rice, if desired.

▶ **MAKES 6 SERVINGS**

flavor variations

● PINEAPPLE CHUTNEY
Combine 2 cups chopped pineapple, 1 tablespoon white vinegar, ¼ teaspoon **Ground Cumin,** ¼ teaspoon **Curry Powder,** pinch **Ground Ginger,** pinch **Ground Red Pepper** and ¼ teaspoon **Cilantro Leaves.** Cover and refrigerate 1 hour to allow flavors to blend.

● GINGERED JASMINE RICE
Cook jasmine rice according to package directions, adding 1 teaspoon **Ground Ginger** to cooking water.

Chicken-Vegetable Stir-Fry

PREP TIME: 15 minutes · **COOK TIME:** 20 minutes

2 tablespoons cornstarch
½ teaspoon **Garlic Powder**
¼ teaspoon **Ground Ginger**
1 pound chicken tenders, cut into 1-inch
    pieces
¼ cup lite soy sauce
¼ cup low-sodium chicken (or vegetable) broth
¼ cup chopped scallions
¼ teaspoon **Crushed Red Pepper,** optional
1 tablespoon canola oil
3 cups vegetables, such as broccoli florets,
    snow peas, red bell pepper strips, sliced
    mushrooms, etc.
2 tablespoons **Sesame Seed,** toasted
    (see below)

1 **MIX** cornstarch with Garlic Powder and Ground Ginger in large bowl. Add chicken; toss to coat well. Set aside. Mix soy sauce, broth, scallions and Crushed Red Pepper. Set aside.

2 **HEAT** oil in wok or large deep skillet on high heat. Add vegetables; stir-fry 5 to 7 minutes or until vegetables are tender-crisp. Remove from pan and set aside.

3 **ADD** chicken and cook 8 to 10 minutes. Add reserved soy sauce mixture. Bring to a boil and cook until sauce has thickened. Return vegetables to skillet, toss. Sprinkle with toasted Sesame Seed. Serve over rice, if desired.

► **MAKES 6 SERVINGS**

flavor variations

● **HOISIN CHICKEN STIR-FRY**
Add 2 teaspoons hoisin sauce to soy sauce mixture. Prepare as directed.

● **VEGGIE STIR-FRY**
Use 2 packages (14 ounces each) extra-firm tofu, cut into 1-inch cubes, in place of chicken. Prepare as directed.

● **TOASTED SESAME SEED**
Heat small skillet on medium heat. Add **Sesame Seed;** cook and stir about 2 minutes or until fragrant and golden brown. Immediately pour out of hot pan to avoid over-toasting.

Lemon-Pepper Chicken Kabobs

PREP TIME: 15 minutes · MARINATE TIME: 30 minutes · COOK TIME: 6 minutes

2 tablespoons cider vinegar
2 tablespoons orange juice concentrate
2 tablespoons soy sauce
½ teaspoon **Lemon Pepper**
½ teaspoon salt
¼ teaspoon **Ground Cinnamon**
1 pound boneless, skinless chicken breasts,
  cut into 1-inch cubes
2 large bell peppers, seeded and cut into
  1-inch squares
1 large onion, peeled and cut into wedges
½ cup chopped scallions

Spiced Fruit Couscous, for serving
  (recipe follows)

1 **COMBINE** vinegar, orange juice concentrate, soy sauce, Lemon Pepper, salt and Ground Cinnamon in large resealable plastic bag. Add chicken and bell pepper and onion pieces. Seal bag and knead until chicken is coated with marinade. Refrigerate 30 minutes or up to 2 hours. Remove chicken from bag; discard marinade.

2 **ASSEMBLE** kabobs, alternating chicken with bell pepper and onion pieces.

3 **GRILL** kabobs 6 minutes or until chicken is marked and cooked through. Sprinkle with chopped scallions and serve.

► **MAKES 4 SERVINGS**

. . . .

flavor variations

. . . .

● SPICED FRUIT COUSCOUS
Heat 2 cups low-sodium chicken broth, 2 teaspoons **Minced Onion** and ½ cup dried apricots over medium heat; bring to a boil. Stir in 1 cup couscous. Return to a boil, cover and turn off heat. Let stand while grilling chicken.

● SHRIMP KABOBS
Use 1 pound peeled and deveined shimp in place of chicken. Marinate 30 minutes. Grill 2 minutes on each side or until shrimp is opaque.

● BLACK PEPPER CHICKEN KABOBS
Substitute ½ teaspoon **Coarse Ground Black Pepper** for Lemon Pepper. Prepare as above.

Slow-Cooker Chicken-Tomato Stew

PREP TIME: 15 minutes · COOK TIME: Slow cooker, LOW, 7 hours; HIGH, 4 hours

1½ pounds boneless, skinless chicken breasts, cut into 1-inch cubes
3 carrots, peeled and sliced
2 ribs celery, trimmed and cubed
1 medium onion, diced
1 medium bell pepper, cored, seeded and diced
1 small zucchini, diced
1 can (14½ ounces) chopped tomatoes
1 **Bay Leaf**
1 teaspoon **Garlic Powder**
1 teaspoon **Basil Leaves**
½ teaspoon **Oregano Leaves**
½ teaspoon salt
½ teaspoon **Ground Black Pepper**

Pasta or couscous, for serving (optional)

1 **PLACE** chicken, carrots, celery, onion, bell pepper and zucchini in slow cooker.

2 **MIX** tomatoes, Bay Leaf, Garlic Powder, Basil Leaves, Oregano Leaves, salt and Ground Black Pepper. Pour tomato mixture over chicken and vegetables.

3 **COVER** and cook on LOW, following manufacturer's directions, for 7 hours or until chicken is tender. Serve over pasta or couscous, if desired.

▶ **MAKES 6 SERVINGS**

flavor variations

● **BAKED CHICKEN-TOMATO STEW**
Prepare as above, assembling dish in 9x13-inch baking dish. Cover and bake in preheated 350°F oven 1 hour or until chicken is tender.

● **GREEK CHICKEN-TOMATO STEW**
Substitute 1 teaspoon **Marjoram Leaves** for Basil Leaves. Prepare as directed.

● **PROVENÇAL CHICKEN-TOMATO STEW**
Substitute ½ teaspoon **Rosemary Leaves** and ½ teaspoon **Thyme Leaves** for Basil Leaves. Prepare as directed.

Spicy Chicken Meatballs

PREP TIME: 20 minutes · COOK TIME: 20 minutes

1½ pounds ground chicken
½ cup unseasoned breadcrumbs
3 tablespoons **Minced Onion**
3 teaspoons **Parsley Flakes**, divided
1 teaspoon **Basil Leaves**
½ teaspoon **Ground Red Pepper**
½ teaspoon salt
1 large egg
3 tablespoons olive oil
½ cup milk
½ cup water
1 package **Chicken Gravy Mix**

Cooked rice or egg noodles, for serving

1 **COMBINE** ground chicken, breadcrumbs, Minced Onion, 1 teaspoon Parsley Flakes, Basil Leaves, Ground Red Pepper and salt in medium bowl until blended. Add egg and thoroughly blend in. Form mixture into 1-inch balls.

2 **HEAT** oil in large nonstick skillet over medium heat. Cook meatballs 10 minutes, turning frequently, until cooked through. Pour fat from pan.

3 **ADD** milk and water to pan. Increase heat to medium-high. Stir in Chicken Gravy Mix and bring to a boil. Lower heat and simmer 1 minute. Return meatballs to pan and cook 1 minute. Stir in remaining 2 teaspoons Parsley Flakes and serve over cooked rice or egg noodles.

► **MAKES 6 SERVINGS**

. . . .

flavor variations
. . . .

● **MEATLOAF MEATBALLS**
Use 1½ pounds ground beef in place of ground chicken. Substitute 4 tablespoons **Meatloaf Seasoning Mix** for Minced Onion, Parsley Flakes, Basil Leaves and Ground Red Pepper. Substitute **Beef Gravy Mix** for Chicken Gravy Mix. Prepare as directed.

● **SPICY PARMESAN MEATBALLS**
Add ¼ cup grated Parmesan cheese to meatballs with breadcrumbs. Prepare as directed.

● **SPICY TURKEY MEATBALLS**
Use 1½ pounds ground turkey in place of ground chicken. Prepare as directed.

Rosemary Roasted Chicken

PREP TIME: 5 minutes · COOK TIME: 1½ hours

2 teaspoons **Rosemary Leaves**
2 teaspoons **Seasoned Salt**
½ teaspoon **Thyme Leaves**
1 tablespoon olive oil
1 whole chicken (3 to 3½ pounds)

Perfect Chicken Gravy, for serving
  (recipe follows)

1 **MIX** Rosemary Leaves, Seasoned Salt and Thyme Leaves in small bowl. Rub oil all over chicken. Sprinkle seasoning mixture over chicken. Place on rack in roasting pan.

2 **ROAST** in preheated 375°F oven 1 to 1½ hours until chicken is cooked through (internal temperature of breast reaches 170°F and thigh is 180°F). Serve with Perfect Chicken Gravy.

► **MAKES 6 SERVINGS**

flavor variations

● **PERFECT CHICKEN GRAVY**
Pour ½ cup drippings from roasting pan and 1½ cups water into medium saucepan. Stir in 2 packages **Chicken Gravy Mix.** Stirring frequently, cook on medium heat until gravy comes to boil. Reduce heat to low; simmer 1 minute or until slightly thickened. (Gravy will thicken upon standing.)

● **SAGE AND LEMON ROASTED CHICKEN**
Substitute 2 teaspoons **Rubbed Sage** for Rosemary Leaves. Place ½ lemon in cavity of chicken. Prepare as directed.

Arroz con Pollo

PREP TIME: 15 minutes · **COOK TIME:** 40 minutes

1 teaspoon salt
¼ teaspoon **Paprika**
¼ teaspoon **Ground Black Pepper**
3 ½ pounds chicken parts, skin removed
1 tablespoon olive oil
1 red bell pepper, cut into 2-inch strips
1 onion, coarsely chopped
1 cup long grain rice
2 cloves garlic, minced
1 can (14 ½ ounces) chicken broth
¼ teaspoon **Saffron**, crushed
1 cup frozen peas
¼ cup sliced Spanish olives with pimientos
  (optional)

1 **MIX** salt, Paprika and Ground Black Pepper. Coat chicken evenly with seasoning mixture.

2 **HEAT** oil in large skillet on medium heat. Add chicken; cook 5 to 6 minutes per side or until golden. Remove chicken from skillet. Pour off all but 1 tablespoon fat from skillet. Add bell pepper and onion; cook, stirring, 5 minutes or until tender.

3 **STIR** in rice and garlic; cook, stirring, 1 minute. Stir in broth and Saffron. Bring to a boil. Return chicken to skillet. Reduce heat to low; cover and simmer 20 minutes or until chicken is cooked through and rice is tender. Remove from heat. Stir in peas; cover. Let stand 5 minutes before serving. Garnish with olives, if desired.

▶ **MAKES 6 SERVINGS**

flavor variations

● **CHICKEN WITH SAFFRON RICE AND CHORIZO**
Add ½ cup chopped chorizo to pan with bell pepper and onion. Prepare as directed.

● **CHICKEN WITH SPICY SAFFRON RICE**
Add ½ teaspoon **Crushed Red Pepper** with broth and Saffron. Prepare as directed.

Balsamic-Roasted Boneless Chicken Thighs

PREP TIME: 10 minutes · MARINATE TIME: 30 minutes · COOK TIME: 20 minutes

½ cup balsamic vinegar
¼ cup olive oil
1 teaspoon **Rosemary Leaves**
1 teaspoon **Basil Leaves**
½ teaspoon **Thyme Leaves**
6 boneless, skinless chicken thighs
   (1½ pounds)
½ teaspoon salt
½ teaspoon **Pepper Medley Grinder**

1 **MIX** balsamic vinegar with olive oil, Rosemary Leaves, Basil Leaves and Thyme Leaves in large resealable plastic bag. Add chicken and knead bag until chicken is coated. Refrigerate chicken in bag 30 minutes. Remove chicken from bag; discard marinade. Place chicken on rimmed baking sheet. Season with salt and Pepper Medley Grinder.

2 **ROAST** in preheated 375°F oven 20 minutes or until cooked through.

► MAKES 6 SERVINGS

. . . .
flavor variations
. . . .

● BALSAMIC-ROASTED
   BONE-IN CHICKEN THIGHS
Use 2½ pounds bone-in chicken thighs in place of boneless chicken thighs. Bake 25 to 30 minutes.

● ITALIAN BALSAMIC-ROASTED
   CHICKEN THIGHS
Substitute 1 tablespoon **Italian Seasoning** for Rosemary Leaves, Basil Leaves and Thyme Leaves. Prepare as directed.

● SUPREME BALSAMIC-ROASTED
   CHICKEN THIGHS
Substitute 1 tablespoon **Salad Supreme**® **Seasoning** for Rosemary Leaves, Basil Leaves and Thyme Leaves. Prepare as directed.

Baked Mustard-Coated Chicken Legs and Thighs

PREP TIME: 15 minutes · MARINATE TIME: 15 minutes · COOK TIME: 30 minutes

1 cup lite soy sauce
½ cup honey
2 tablespoons vegetable oil
3 tablespoons **Ground Mustard,** divided
2 to 3 pounds chicken leg and thigh quarters
1½ cups unseasoned breadcrumbs
1 teaspoon **Paprika**
¼ teaspoon salt
½ teaspoon **Ground Black Pepper**

1 **MIX** soy sauce, honey, oil, 1 tablespoon Ground Mustard in a resealable plastic bag. Add chicken, seal and push chicken around to coat evenly. Refrigerate 15 minutes. Remove chicken from bag, brushing off any excess marinade; discard marinade.

2 **STIR** breadcrumbs, remaining 2 tablespoons Ground Mustard, Paprika, salt and Ground Black Pepper in shallow bowl. Roll chicken in breadcrumb mixture. Place chicken in single layer on rimmed baking sheet. Spray chicken with nonstick cooking spray.

3 **BAKE** in preheated 350°F oven 25 to 30 minutes or until cooked through.

► **MAKES 6 SERVINGS**

flavor variations

● **GRILLED MUSTARD-COATED CHICKEN**
Preheat grill to medium-high heat. Prepare chicken as above. Grill over direct heat, skin side down, until cooked through, 10 to 12 minutes per side.

● **MUSTARD-TARRAGON CHICKEN**
Substitute 1 teaspoon **Tarragon Leaves** for Paprika. Prepare as directed.

● **MONTREAL-MUSTARD CHICKEN**
Substitute 1 teaspoon **Grill Mates®** **Montreal Chicken Seasoning** for Paprika. Prepare as above.

Baked Provençal Chicken Thighs

PREP TIME: 15 minutes · **COOK TIME:** 45 minutes

6 boneless, skinless chicken thighs
   (1½ pounds)
1 large onion, peeled and sliced
1 red bell pepper, cored, seeded and sliced
1 can (14½ ounces) chopped tomatoes
1 cup pitted black olives, drained
1 teaspoon **Garlic Powder**
1 teaspoon **Thyme Leaves**
½ teaspoon salt
¼ teaspoon **Ground Red Pepper**

1 **PLACE** chicken thighs in single layer in baking dish. Top with onion and bell pepper.

2 **COMBINE** remaining ingredients in medium bowl; stir to mix. Pour mixture over chicken.

3 **COVER** and bake in preheated 400°F oven 45 minutes or until chicken is cooked through.

► **MAKES 6 SERVINGS**

flavor variations

● **SLOW-COOKER PROVENÇAL CHICKEN THIGHS**
Place chicken in slow cooker. Add onion and bell pepper. Combine remaining ingredients in medium bowl and pour over chicken. Cover and cook on LOW 7 hours or until chicken is tender.

● **ROSEMARY CHICKEN THIGHS**
Add 1 teaspoon **Rosemary Leaves** and ½ teaspoon **Celery Seed** to tomato mixture. Prepare as directed.

● **GREEK CHICKEN THIGHS**
Substitute 1 teaspoon **Oregano Leaves** for Thyme Leaves. Use 1 cup pitted kalamata olives in place of black olives. Prepare as directed.

Chicken Adobado Tacos

PREP TIME: 15 minutes · COOK TIME: 15 minutes

1 tablespoon vegetable oil
1 can (3½ ounces) chopped green chiles
1 medium onion, peeled and chopped
1 teaspoon **Garlic Powder**
1 can (14½ ounces) chopped tomatoes
1 tablespoon tomato paste
½ cup water
1 package **Taco Seasoning Mix**
3 cups shredded rotisserie chicken
Corn or flour tortillas, for serving

1 **HEAT** oil in large nonstick skillet over medium heat. Add green chiles, onion and Garlic Powder and cook 2 minutes. Stir in canned tomatoes, tomato paste, water and Taco Seasoning Mix; cook 1 minute.

2 **STIR** in chicken. Cook 10 minutes, until most of liquid has evaporated. Serve with warmed corn or flour tortillas.

▶ **MAKES 6 SERVINGS**

flavor variations

● TACO ACCOMPANIMENTS
Serve tacos with 3 cups shredded iceberg lettuce, 1½ cups diced fresh plum tomatoes, 1 cup diced red onion, 1 cup shredded Monterey Jack or Cheddar cheese, 1 cup sour cream and salsa.

● QUICK SALSA
Combine 4 chopped plum tomatoes, 1 teaspoon **Cilantro Leaves,** ½ chopped red onion and ½ seeded and diced jalapeño. Stir in juice of 1 lime and ½ teaspoon salt.

Chicken Enchilada Bake

PREP TIME: 15 minutes · COOK TIME: 15 minutes

1 package **Enchilada Sauce Mix**
1½ cups water
1 can (8 ounces) tomato sauce
1 can (3½ ounces) chopped green chiles
4 cups shredded cooked chicken
12 corn tortillas, cut into quarters
1 large onion, peeled and chopped
1½ cups grated Monterey Jack cheese
Sour cream, chopped scallions and sliced olives, for serving

1 STIR Enchilada Sauce Mix and water in medium saucepan. Add tomato sauce and green chiles. Bring to boil over medium-high heat. Reduce heat and simmer, stirring occasionally, 5 minutes or until thick. Remove from heat. Stir in chicken.

2 PLACE one-third of tortilla pieces in bottom of lightly greased 9x13-inch baking dish. Top with one-third of chicken mixture. Sprinkle with one-third of onions and ½ cup cheese. Repeat each layer twice, ending with cheese.

3 BROIL 5 to 8 minutes or until golden and bubbling.

► MAKES 6 SERVINGS

flavor variations

● TURKEY ENCHILADA BAKE
Use 3 cups shredded cooked turkey in place of chicken. Prepare as directed.

● PORK ENCHILADA BAKE
Use 3 cups shredded cooked pork shoulder in place of chicken. Prepare as directed.

● PEPPER JACK–CHICKEN ENCHILADA BAKE
Use 1 cup shredded pepper Jack in place of 1 cup Monterey Jack. Prepare as directed.

● CHICKEN TACO BAKE
Substitute 1 package **Taco Seasoning Mix** for Enchilada Sauce Mix. Prepare as directed.

Chicken-Broccoli Pot Pie

PREP TIME: 20 minutes · COOK TIME: 40 minutes

1 package **Chicken Gravy Mix**
½ teaspoon **Poultry Seasoning**
2 cups diced cooked chicken breast
1 cup broccoli florets
1 package (**15 ounces**) refrigerated
   pie crusts (**2 crusts**)
2 cups shredded Swiss cheese, divided
4 ounces smoked ham, diced

1 **PREPARE** Chicken Gravy Mix according to package directions for "Creamy Gravy." Stir in Poultry Seasoning. Add chicken and broccoli and toss to mix.

2 **UNFOLD** pie crust into pie plate. Spoon 1¼ cups chicken mixture in bottom of crust. Sprinkle with 1 cup cheese, cover with ham and sprinkle with remaining cheese. Top with remaining chicken mixture. Cover filling with pastry top. Press crust edges together to seal crust.

3 **BAKE** in preheated 400°F oven 40 to 45 minutes or until crust is golden brown. Remove from oven and let stand 5 minutes before serving.

► **MAKES 6 SERVINGS**

flavor variations

● **TURKEY AND SWISS POT PIE**
Use 6 thin slices of smoked turkey in place of ham <u>and</u> 2 cups diced cooked turkey breast in place of chicken. Prepare as directed.

● **MAKE-AHEAD POT PIE**
Prepare pie as directed, but do not bake. Wrap tightly in plastic wrap. Refrigerate up to 8 hours or freeze up to 1 month. Bake frozen pie in preheated 400°F oven 1 hour 15 minutes.

● **CHICKEN-BROCCOLI POT PIE**
   WITH CHEDDAR
Use 2 cups shredded Cheddar cheese in place of Swiss cheese. Prepare as directed.

Chicken Salad

PREP TIME: 15 minutes · REFRIGERATE: 30 minutes

½ cup plain low-fat yogurt
2 tablespoons mayonnaise
1 teaspoon **Parsley Flakes**
½ teaspoon **Seasoned Salt**
¼ teaspoon **Ground Black Pepper**
2 cups cubed cooked chicken
½ cup thinly sliced celery
¼ cup chopped red onion

Sliced bread or salad greens, for serving

1 **MIX** yogurt, mayonnaise, Parsley Flakes, Seasoned Salt and Ground Black Pepper in large bowl until combined. Add chicken, celery and onion; toss to coat well. Cover.

2 **REFRIGERATE** at least 30 minutes or until ready to serve. Serve in a sandwich or on salad greens.

▶ **MAKES 6 SERVINGS**

• •
flavor variations
• •

● **FRUITY CHICKEN SALAD**
Add ½ cup fresh or dried fruit, such as chopped dried apricots, chopped apple <u>or</u> halved grapes to the chicken salad. Prepare as directed.

● **NUTTY CHICKEN SALAD**
Add ¼ cup chopped nuts such as pistachios, pecans or walnuts. Prepare as directed.

● **ALMOND CHICKEN SALAD**
Add ¼ teaspoon **Ground Ginger** to mayonnaise mixture. Add ½ cup golden raisins and ¼ cup toasted slivered almonds with chicken. Prepare as directed.

● **CURRIED CHICKEN SALAD**
Add 1 teaspoon **Curry Powder** and ½ teaspoon **Ground Cinnamon** to mayonnaise mixture. Add ½ cup dried cranberries and ¼ cup toasted slivered almonds with chicken. Prepare as directed.

Tuscan Chicken Salad

PREP TIME: 15 minutes

1 pound cooked chicken breast meat, diced
1 small red onion, peeled and cut into thin
  strips
1 large tomato, chopped
1 can (15.5 ounces) chickpeas, rinsed and
  drained
1 teaspoon **Basil Leaves**
Balsamic Vinaigrette (recipe follows)
1 bag (5 ounces) mixed salad greens

1 **COMBINE** chicken, onion, tomato, chickpeas and Basil Leaves in large bowl. Add Balsamic Vinaigrette and toss to mix.

2 **PILE** salad greens in serving bowl. Scoop chicken mixture over greens. Serve immediately.

► **MAKES 6 SERVINGS**

flavor variations

● **BALSAMIC VINAIGRETTE**
Combine 3 tablespoons balsamic vinegar, ½ teaspoon Dijon mustard, ½ teaspoon **Basil Leaves** and ½ teaspoon **Oregano Leaves** in small bowl. Gradually add ½ cup extra-virgin olive oil, whisking constantly. Season with ¼ teaspoon <u>each</u> salt <u>and</u> **Ground Black Pepper.**

● **TUSCAN CHICKEN SALAD WITH SPINACH**
Use 8 cups baby spinach in place of mixed salad greens. Prepare as directed.

● **TUSCAN CHICKEN SALAD WITH WHITE BEANS**
Use 2 cups white beans in place of chickpeas. Prepare as directed.

Simple Turkey Mole with Guacamole

PREP TIME: 15 minutes · COOK TIME: 1 hour

1 pound boneless turkey breast, cut into
   ½-inch cubes
1½ cups diced onions
1 cup diced red bell pepper
¾ cup water
1 package **Taco Seasoning Mix**
1 tablespoon grated bittersweet chocolate
1 teaspoon **Ground Cumin**
1 teaspoon **Oregano Leaves**
1 teaspoon **Ground Cinnamon**
½ teaspoon **Garlic Powder**

Rice and warm tortillas, for serving
Guacamole, for serving (recipe follows)

1 **COMBINE** turkey, onions and bell pepper in large ovenproof soup pot. Add water, Taco Seasoning Mix, grated chocolate, Ground Cumin, Oregano Leaves, Ground Cinnamon and Garlic Powder; stir. Cover.

2 **BAKE** in preheated 350°F oven 1 hour or until turkey is tender. Serve over rice with warm tortillas and Guacamole on the side.

► MAKES 4 SERVINGS

flavor variations

● GUACAMOLE
Place 2 medium ripe peeled and seeded avocados, juice of 1 lime, 1 teaspoon **Cilantro Leaves** and ⅛ teaspoon **Ground Cumin** in medium bowl. Mash with fork until mostly smooth. Serve immediately or sprinkle with lime juice, cover with plastic wrap (pressed directly on the surface) and refrigerate until ready to use.

● SLOW-COOKER TURKEY MOLE
Combine all ingredients in a slow cooker. Cook on LOW 5 hours or until turkey and vegetables are tender.

● TURKEY MOLE ENCHILADAS
Prepare as directed. Roll ⅛ cup cooked turkey mixture in each of 12 corn tortillas and place in single layer in greased 9x13-inch baking dish. Spoon remaining mole over rolled tortillas and sprinkle with 1 cup Monterey Jack cheese. Bake in preheated 350°F oven 10 minutes or until cheese is melted.

Turkey Satay with Peanut Sauce

PREP TIME: 15 minutes · MARINATE TIME: 1 hour · COOK TIME: 6 minutes

½ cup peanut butter
½ cup hot water
1 tablespoon low-sodium soy sauce
1 tablespoon lime juice
1½ teaspoon **Ground Ginger**
½ teaspoon **Ground Cinnamon**
½ teaspoon **Crushed Red Pepper**
1 pound boneless, skinless turkey breast,
   cut crosswise into ¾-inch thick strips

1 **MIX** peanut butter, water, soy sauce, lime juice, Ground Ginger, Ground Cinnamon and Crushed Red Pepper in small bowl. Reserve one-third of peanut sauce for dipping. Place turkey in 9x13-inch baking dish. Pour remaining sauce over top and toss to coat evenly. Cover dish with plastic wrap. Refrigerate at least 1 hour or up to 24 hours. Remove turkey from marinade; thread 1 piece onto each of 16 skewers. Discard marinade.

2 **HEAT** grill pan over medium-high heat until hot but not smoking. Cook several pieces of turkey at a time, 3 minutes per side or until cooked through. Keep warm.

3 **HEAT** reserved peanut sauce in small saucepan over medium heat. Bring to a simmer and remove from heat. Serve turkey with peanut sauce.

► MAKES 4 SERVINGS

flavor variations

● BAKED TURKEY SATAY
Prepare as directed but do not grill. Bake satay in preheated 450°F oven for 6 minutes, turning occasionally, or until cooked through.

● CHICKEN SATAY
Use 1 pound boneless, skinless chicken breasts in place of turkey. Prepare as directed.

● SPICY TURKEY SATAY
Add ¼ teaspoon **Ground Red Pepper** to peanut sauce before marinating turkey. Prepare as directed.

Turkey with Spiced Soy Glaze

PREP TIME: 15 minutes · MARINATE TIME: 1 hour · COOK TIME: 22 minutes

½ cup low-sodium soy sauce
3 tablespoons honey
1 tablespoon orange juice
½ teaspoon **Ground Ginger**
½ teaspoon **Pumpkin Pie Spice**
1 teaspoon oil
4 turkey cutlets (6 ounces <u>each</u>)
½ teaspoon salt
½ teaspoon **Ground Black Pepper**

1 **WHISK** together soy sauce, honey, orange juice, Ground Ginger and Pumpkin Pie Spice in small bowl.

2 **HEAT** oil in large nonstick skillet over medium heat. Add turkey and cook, turning once, 12 minutes or until cooked through. Remove turkey from pan and keep warm.

3 **ADD** soy sauce mixture to skillet and bring to a boil. Cook 5 minutes or until sauce has thickened. Return turkey to pan and cook 5 minutes or until heated through and sauce has reduced to a glaze.

▶ **MAKES 4 SERVINGS**

flavor variations

● **CHICKEN WITH SPICED SOY GLAZE**
Use 4 boneless, skinless chicken breasts in place of turkey. Prepare as directed.

● **TURKEY WITH APPLE-SPICE SOY GLAZE**
Substitute ¼ teaspoon **Apple Pie Spice** for the Pumpkin Pie Spice. Prepare as directed.

Turkey-Spinach Shepherd's Pie

PREP TIME: 15 minutes · COOK TIME: 50 minutes

2 pounds ground turkey
¾ cup breadcrumbs
½ cup chopped spinach (if using frozen, drain well)
½ teaspoon **Ground Thyme**
½ teaspoon **Poultry Seasoning**
¼ teaspoon **Ground Red Pepper**
½ teaspoon salt
2½ cups prepared mashed potatoes

1 **COMBINE** turkey, breadcrumbs, spinach, Ground Thyme, Poultry Seasoning and Ground Red Pepper in medium bowl. Season with salt. Mound the mixture into glass pie plate. Spoon mashed potatoes on top, smoothing them to completely cover meat. Spray with nonstick vegetable spray.

2 **BAKE** in preheated 375°F oven 50 minutes or until top is golden brown and interior is cooked through.

▶ **MAKES 6 SERVINGS**

flavor variations

● TURKEY SHEPHERD'S PIE
   WITH PEAS AND CARROTS
Use ½ cup frozen mixed peas and carrots, thawed and drained, in place of spinach. Prepare as directed.

● CHICKEN-SPINACH SHEPHERD'S PIE
Use 2 pounds ground chicken in place of turkey. Prepare as directed.

● THYME-SAGE TURKEY SHEPHERD'S PIE
Substitute ½ teaspoon **Ground Sage** for Poultry Seasoning. Prepare as directed.

Montreal Turkey Burgers

PREP TIME: 5 minutes · **COOK TIME:** 12 minutes

1 pound ground turkey
1 tablespoon **Grill Mates® Montreal Chicken Seasoning**
4 hamburger rolls

Lettuce, tomato, onion and condiments, for serving

1 **MIX** ground turkey and Chicken Seasoning in medium bowl until blended. Shape into 4 patties.

2 **GRILL** over medium heat 4 to 6 minutes per side or until burgers are cooked through (internal temperature reaches 160°F). Toast rolls open side down on grill about 30 seconds or until golden. Serve burgers on toasted rolls with desired toppings and condiments.

► **MAKES 4 TO 6 SERVINGS**

flavor variations

● SPICY MONTREAL TURKEY BURGERS
Substitute 1 tablespoon **Grill Mates® Spicy Montreal Steak Seasoning** for Chicken Seasoning.

● LEMON-PEPPER BURGERS
Substitute 1 tablespoon **Lemon Pepper** for Montreal Chicken Seasoning.

BBQ Turkey Meatloaf

PREP TIME: 15 minutes · **COOK TIME:** 1 hour

2 pounds ground turkey
1 cup finely diced onion
1 cup barbecue sauce, divided
1 large egg
¾ cup breadcrumbs
2 tablespoons **Grill Mates® Montreal Chicken Seasoning**
1 tablespoon Worcestershire Sauce

1 **MIX** turkey, onion and ½ cup barbecue sauce in medium bowl until blended. Add egg and mix until blended. Add breadcrumbs and Chicken Seasoning; mix again until blended. Form meat into loaf shape and place in 8x5-inch baking dish.

2 **BAKE** in preheated 375°F oven 45 minutes. Pour remaining ½ cup barbecue sauce over meatloaf and bake 15 minutes or until cooked through. Remove from oven and let stand 10 minutes before cutting into slices and serving.

➤ **MAKES 6 SERVINGS**

flavor variations

● **BBQ MEATLOAF**
Use 2 pounds ground beef in place of turkey. Prepare as directed.

● **MESQUITE BBQ MEATLOAF**
Substitute 1 tablespoon **Grill Mates® Mesquite Seasoning** for Chicken Seasoning. Prepare as directed.

Beef & Pork

Sweet 'n' Spicy Slow-Cooker Chili

PREP TIME: 10 minutes · COOK TIME: LOW, 8 hours; HIGH, 4 hours

2 pounds ground beef
½ cup chopped onion
1 tablespoon **California Style® Wet Garlic**
2 cans (14½ ounces <u>each</u>) tomatoes with
    diced green chiles
1 can (15 ounces) white hominy, drained
1 package **Mild Chili Seasoning**
2 teaspoons **Cinnamon Sugar**
1 teaspoon cocoa powder
½ teaspoon salt

Shredded cheese, sour cream and
    chopped onion, for serving

1 COMBINE beef, onion, Wet Garlic, tomatoes, hominy, Chili Seasoning, Cinnamon Sugar, cocoa powder and salt in slow cooker.

2 COOK on LOW 8 hours or HIGH 4 hours. Serve hot topped with shredded cheese, sour cream and chopped onion, if desired.

► MAKES 8 SERVINGS

flavor variations

● SWEET 'N' HOT SLOW-COOKER CHILI
Substitute **Hot Chili Seasoning** for
Mild Chili Seasoning. Prepare as directed.

● SWEET 'N' SPICY TURKEY CHILI
Use 2 pounds ground turkey in place of
ground beef. Prepare as directed.

● SWEET 'N' SPICY CORN CHILI
Omit hominy; prepare chili as above. Stir
in 1 can (15 ounces) kernel corn, drained,
just before serving.

All-American Burgers

PREP TIME: 10 minutes · **COOK TIME:** 12 minutes

1 pound ground beef
¼ cup ketchup
1 tablespoon **Grill Mates® Hamburger Seasoning**
1 teaspoon Worcestershire sauce
4 slices Cheddar or American cheese
4 hamburger rolls
8 slices cooked bacon (optional)

Lettuce, tomato and condiments, for serving

1 **MIX** ground beef, ketchup, Hamburger Seasoning and Worcestershire sauce in large bowl. Form mixture into four ½-inch-thick patties.

2 **GRILL** burgers over medium heat 4 to 6 minutes per side or until cooked through. Add cheese slices to burgers 1 minute before cooking is completed. Toast rolls open side down on grill, about 30 seconds. Serve burgers with bacon slices, if desired, on toasted rolls. Garnish with desired toppings and condiments.

▶ **MAKES 4 SERVINGS**

flavor variations

● CANADIAN BURGERS
Prepare as directed. Omit bacon slices. Grill 4 slices Canadian bacon just until lightly marked. Top each burger with a slice of Canadian bacon before serving.

● SPICY BACON CHEESEBURGERS
Substitute 1 tablespoon **Grill Mates® Spicy Montreal Steak Seasoning** for the Hamburger Seasoning. Prepare burgers as directed. Omit the Cheddar or American cheese; top each burger with 1 slice pepper Jack cheese.

Jerk Burgers

PREP TIME: 15 minutes · COOK TIME: 15 minutes

¼ cup **Minced Onion**
2 tablespoons **Parsley Flakes**
1 tablespoon **Ground Mustard**
2 teaspoons **Ground Cinnamon**
1 teaspoon **Ground Allspice**
1 teaspoon **Ground Red Pepper**
½ teaspoon **Garlic Powder**
½ teaspoon **Oregano Leaves**
½ teaspoon **Celery Salt**
¼ teaspoon salt
1 pound ground round steak

Mango Salsa, for serving (recipe follows)
Sliced scallions, for garnish, optional

1 **STIR** Minced Onion, Parsley Flakes, Ground Mustard, Ground Cinnamon, Allspice, Ground Red Pepper, Garlic Powder, Oregano Leaves, Celery Salt and salt in small bowl until blended.

2 **COMBINE** ground round with 2 teaspoons seasoning mix. Form mixture into four ½-inch-thick patties. Dust with additional seasoning mix. (You will have seasoning mix left over.)

3 **GRILL** over medium-high heat, turning occasionally, 7 to 8 minutes per side or until cooked through. Serve with Mango Salsa and sliced scallions, if desired.

► **MAKES 4 SERVINGS**

flavor variations

● **MAKE-AHEAD SEASONING MIX**
The seasoning mix will keep, tightly covered, up to 3 months. You can use it with chicken breasts, ground turkey or pork, or shrimp.

● **MANGO SALSA**
Mix ½ cup chopped mango, 2 tablespoons diced red bell pepper, 3 tablespoons diced red onion and ⅛ teaspoon **Ground Red Pepper** in small bowl. Stir in 1 tablespoon chopped scallions, if desired.

Pizza Meatloaf

PREP TIME: 10 minutes · COOK TIME: 1 hour

1½ pounds lean ground beef
¾ cup breadcrumbs
1 cup chopped mushrooms
½ cup canned chopped tomatoes, well-drained
3 tablespoons **Minced Onion**
1 tablespoon **Parsley Flakes**
1½ teaspoons **Italian Seasoning**
½ teaspoon salt
½ teaspoon **Ground Black Pepper**
1 jar (6 ounces) pizza sauce
1 cup shredded Mozzarella cheese

1 **MIX** ground beef, breadcrumbs, mushrooms, tomatoes, Minced Onion, Parsley Flakes, Italian Seasoning, salt and Ground Black Pepper in large bowl. Form mixture into loaf shape and place in 8x5-inch baking pan. Pour pizza sauce over loaf.

2 **BAKE** in preheated 350°F oven 55 minutes. Top with shredded cheese and bake 5 minutes or until cheese is melted. Let stand 5 minutes before slicing.

▶ **MAKES 6 SERVINGS**

flavor variations

● **TURKEY PIZZA MEATLOAF**
Use ground turkey in place of ground beef. Prepare as directed.

● **MEATLOAF PARMIGIANA**
Use marinara sauce in place of pizza sauce. Prepare as directed.

● **GARLICKY PIZZA MEATLOAF**
Add 1 teaspoon **Minced Garlic** with Minced Onion. Prepare as directed.

Picadillo

PREP TIME: 8 minutes · COOK TIME: 20 minutes

1 pound ground beef
1 cup chopped onion
1 can (14½ ounces) diced tomatoes
½ cup water
1 package **Taco Seasoning Mix**
½ teaspoon **Garlic Powder**
¼ teaspoon **Ground Cinnamon**
⅛ teaspoon **Ground Cloves**
1 jar (2 ounces) pimiento-stuffed green
   olives, drained
½ cup raisins

4 crispy (6-inch) tostadas, for serving
Sliced scallions, for garnish, optional

1 **COOK** beef in large nonstick skillet over medium-high heat, 5 minutes, stirring frequently, until most of the fat has cooked out. Drain off fat.

2 **STIR** in onion, tomatoes, water, Taco Seasoning Mix, Garlic Powder, Ground Cinnamon and Ground Cloves. Reduce heat to medium.

3 **COVER** and simmer 10 minutes. Stir in olives and raisins; cook 5 minutes. To serve, spoon mixture onto crispy tostadas and garnish with sliced scallions, if desired.

▶ **MAKES 4 SERVINGS**

flavor variations

● **TURKEY PICADILLO**
Use ground turkey in place of ground beef. Prepare as directed.

● **PICADILLO SOFT TACOS**
Prepare as directed. Warm 8 (6-inch) corn or flour tortillas. Spoon picadillo on each tortilla, fold over and serve.

● **PICADILLO WITH RICE**
Prepare as directed. Serve over cooked rice.

● **PICADILLO WITH PEPPERS**
Add 1 large green bell pepper, cored, seeded and diced, with onions and tomatoes. Prepare as directed.

● **PICADILLO BURRITOS**
Substitute 1 package **Burrito Seasoning Mix** for Taco Seasoning Mix. To serve, wrap mixture in warm flour tortillas.

Empanadas

PREP TIME: 15 minutes · COOK TIME: 40 minutes

⅓ pound lean ground beef
¼ cup **Minced Onion**
½ teaspoon **Ground Cumin**
¼ teaspoon **Crushed Red Pepper**
¼ teaspoon **Garlic Powder**
⅛ teaspoon **Ground Cinnamon**
2 tablespoons dried cranberries (optional)
2 packages refrigerated pie crusts (4 crusts)
2 tablespoons water
1 egg, stirred with 3 tablespoons water

Salsa and sour cream, for serving

1 **COMBINE** ground beef, Minced Onion, Ground Cumin, Crushed Red Pepper, Garlic Powder and Ground Cinnamon in medium nonstick skillet. Cook over medium heat, stirring frequently, 5 minutes or until mixture has begun to brown. Stir in dried cranberries, if using; cook 3 minutes. Remove from heat.

2 **CUT** four 4-inch circles out of one 9-inch crust. Place an equal amount of meat filling into the center of each circle. Brush cold water around the edge of each circle and fold in half to make crescent-shaped packets, pressing edges closed with fork. Place on nonstick rimmed baking sheet. Brush with egg mixture. Repeat with remaining pastry and filling.

3 **BAKE** in preheated 350°F oven 30 minutes or until pastry is golden brown. Serve hot with salsa and sour cream, if desired.

► **MAKES 8 SERVINGS**

flavor variations

● **EXTRA-CRISPY EMPANADAS**
Prepare as directed. Preheat oven to 450°F. Bake 10 minutes, then reduce oven temperature to 325°F and bake 12 minutes or until golden brown.

● **CARIBBEAN BEEF PATTIES**
Substitute ½ teaspoon **Thyme Leaves,** ¼ teaspoon **Ground Red Pepper,** ¼ teaspoon **Curry Powder,** ⅛ teaspoon **Ground Black Pepper** and ⅛ teaspoon **Ground Allspice** for Ground Cumin, Crushed Red Pepper, Garlic Powder and Ground Cinnamon. Prepare as directed.

Green Chile Tacos

PREP TIME: 15 minutes · COOK TIME: 10 minutes

1 pound lean ground beef
½ cup finely diced red bell pepper
¼ cup finely diced red onion
1 package **Taco Seasoning Mix**
½ cup water
1 tablespoon tomato paste
1 (4-ounce) can chopped green chiles,
   drained

8 warm taco shells or 6-inch corn tortillas,
   for serving
1 cup (4 ounces) shredded Monterey Jack
   cheese, for serving
2 cups shredded lettuce, for serving

1 **COOK** ground beef, bell pepper and onion in large nonstick skillet over medium-high heat, stirring to break up meat, for about 5 minutes or until the meat is browned. Drain fat.

2 **ADD** in Taco Seasoning Mix and stir until blended. Add water and tomato paste; bring to a boil.

3 **COOK,** stirring, 5 minutes or until the mixture has thickened slightly. Stir in chiles. To serve, spoon mixture into warm taco shells or tortillas. Sprinkle with shredded cheese and lettuce.

► MAKES 4 SERVINGS

. . . .

flavor variations

. . . .

● GREEN CHILE TURKEY TACOS
Use ground turkey in place of ground beef.
Prepare as directed.

● GREEN CHILE BEEF BURRITOS
Substitute 1 package **Burrito Seasoning Mix** for **Taco Seasoning Mix.** Prepare ground beef mixture as above. To serve, spoon mixture onto 4 warm 8-inch flour tortillas. Top with shredded lettuce, shredded cheese and sour cream.

Stuffed Acorn Squash with Spiced Beef

PREP TIME: 10 minutes · COOK TIME: 55 minutes

1 pound ground beef
½ cup **Minced Onion**
1 teaspoon **Seasoned Salt**
½ teaspoon **Garlic Powder**
½ teaspoon **Ground Cumin**
¼ teaspoon **Ground Allspice**
¼ teaspoon **Ground Red Pepper**
2 large acorn squash, cut in half from stem
   to blossom end, seeds removed

1 MIX beef, Minced Onion, Seasoned Salt, Garlic Powder, Ground Cumin, Ground Allspice and Ground Red Pepper in medium bowl. Divide mixture evenly among squash halves.

2 PLACE stuffed squash in 9x13-inch baking pan. Spray stuffed squash with nonstick spray. Cover pan with aluminum foil.

3 BAKE in preheated 350°F oven and bake 45 minutes or until squash is tender. Uncover and bake 10 minutes or until filling is browned.

➤ **MAKES 4 SERVINGS**

flavor variations

● STUFFED ACORN SQUASH
   WITH SPICED BEEF AND APPLES
Omit Ground Cumin, Garlic Powder, and Seasoned Salt. Add 1 teaspoon **Apple Pie Spice** to ground beef mixture. Stir in ½ cup diced apple. Prepare as directed.

Pepper Steak

PREP TIME: 10 minutes · **COOK TIME:** 10 minutes

1 package **Pot Roast Seasoning Mix**
¾ cup tomato juice
2 tablespoons soy sauce
1 teaspoon tomato paste
1 teaspoon **Onion Powder**
⅛ teaspoon **Garlic Powder**
2 pounds top round steak, cut into thin strips
1 large onion, cut lengthwise into thin strips
1 large red bell pepper, seeded and cut into thin strips

Cooked rice, for serving

1 **STIR** together Pot Roast Seasoning Mix, tomato juice, soy sauce, tomato paste, Onion Powder and Garlic Powder in small bowl until blended.

2 **HEAT** large nonstick skillet over medium heat. Add steak and cook 2 minutes or until no longer pink. Add onion, bell pepper and seasoning mixture; bring to a boil.

3 **COOK**, stirring occasionally, 6 minutes or until meat is cooked through and sauce is slightly thick. Remove from heat and serve over rice, if desired.

▶ **MAKES 8 SERVINGS**

flavor variations

● **SLOW-COOKER PEPPER STEAK**
Add 2 whole cored and quartered tomatoes and ½ cup thinly sliced celery with the onion and pepper. Add ¼ teaspoon **Ground Red Pepper** to seasoning mixture. Cook in slow cooker 3 hours on HIGH or 6 hours on LOW.

Cuban-Style Shredded Steak

PREP TIME: 15 minutes · COOK TIME: Slow cooker, LOW, 8 hours; HIGH, 4 hours

2½ pounds flank steak, trimmed of all excess fat
1 can (8 ounces) tomato sauce
1 cup low-sodium beef broth
1 package **Taco Seasoning Mix**
1 large onion, diced
1 large red bell pepper, seeded and diced
1 tablespoon **Cilantro Leaves**
1 teaspoon **Ground Black Pepper**
1 tablespoon apple cider vinegar

Cooked rice and black beans, for serving

1 **PLACE** steak in slow cooker. Pour in tomato sauce and beef broth. Add Taco Seasoning Mix, onion, bell pepper, Cilantro Leaves and Ground Black Pepper.

2 **COVER** and cook on LOW 8 hours or on HIGH 4 hours.

3 **SHRED** cooked meat and stir in vinegar. Serve with rice and black beans, if desired.

► MAKES 4 TO 6 SERVINGS

flavor variations

● GARLICKY CUBAN STEAK
Add 1 seeded and diced medium green bell pepper and 1 teaspoon **California Style® Wet Garlic** to slow cooker with seasonings. Prepare as directed.

● STOVETOP CUBAN-STYLE STEAK
Combine all ingredients in large saucepot. Bring to a boil over medium heat; reduce heat to medium-low and cook 2 hours until meat is tender.

Szechuan Beef

PREP TIME: 10 minutes · MARINATE TIME: 1 hour · COOK TIME: 5 minutes

3 tablespoons soy sauce
3 tablespoons sherry
2 tablespoons sesame oil
¼ teaspoon **Ground Ginger**
¼ teaspoon **Garlic Powder**
¼ teaspoon **Ground Cloves**
⅛ teaspoon **Crushed Red Pepper**
1 pound flank steak, cut into thin strips
1 tablespoon peanut oil or vegetable oil
½ green bell pepper, sliced into strips
½ cup shredded carrot
¼ cup chopped scallions
1 tablespoon **Sesame Seed**

Cooked rice, for serving
Spicy Soy Dipping Sauce (recipe follows),
    for serving (optional)

1 **MIX** soy sauce, sherry, sesame oil, Ground Ginger, Garlic Powder, Ground Cloves and Crushed Red Pepper in resealable plastic bag. Add steak, seal and shake bag to coat evenly. Refrigerate 1 hour.

2 **HEAT** peanut oil in wok over high heat. When very hot, add bell pepper and carrot. Stir-fry 1 minute. Remove beef from bag; discard marinade. Stir-fry 4 minutes or until beef is just cooked. Sprinkle with scallions and Sesame Seed. Serve with cooked rice and Spicy Soy Dipping Sauce, if desired.

► **MAKES 4 SERVINGS**

···································

flavor variations

···································

● SZECHUAN CHICKEN
Use 1 pound sliced boneless, skinless chicken breast in place of beef. Prepare as directed.

● SPICY SOY DIPPING SAUCE
Stir together ½ cup soy sauce, 1 tablespoon honey, ¼ teaspoon **Crushed Red Pepper** and ¼ teaspoon **Ground Ginger** until blended. Serve with beef.

Indian-Spiced Beef Kabobs

PREP TIME: 10 minutes · MARINATE TIME: 30 minutes · COOK TIME: 12 minutes

1 cup nonfat plain yogurt
1 tablespoon **Minced Onion**
1 teaspoon **Curry Powder**
1 teaspoon **Ground Cumin**
1 teaspoon **Paprika**
1 teaspoon **Seasoned Salt**
½ teaspoon **Garlic Powder**
¼ teaspoon **Ground Red Pepper**
1 to 1½ pounds beef sirloin, cut into
   1½-inch cubes
Whole-wheat tortillas, for serving, optional

1 **COMBINE** yogurt, Minced Onion, Curry Powder, Ground Cumin, Paprika, Seasoned Salt, Garlic Powder and Ground Red Pepper in resealable plastic bag. Add beef, seal and squeeze bag to coat evenly. Refrigerate 30 minutes. Remove beef from bag; discard marinade.

2 **DIVIDE** beef chunks evenly among 8 metal skewers. Place skewers on rimmed baking sheet (be careful not to crowd the pan or the meat won't brown).

3 **BAKE** in preheated 450°F oven 12 minutes or until edges are browned and crisp and beef is cooked through. Serve hot with whole-wheat tortillas, if desired.

► **MAKES 4 SERVINGS**

flavor variations

● TACO-SPICED BEEF KABOBS
Substitute 1 package **Taco Seasoning Mix** for Curry Powder, Ground Cumin, Paprika, Seasoned Salt and Ground Red Pepper. Prepare as directed.

● MOROCCAN-SPICED BEEF KABOBS
Substitute ½ teaspoon **Ground Cinnamon,** ¼ teaspoon **Ground Black Pepper,** ¼ teaspoon **Ground Cumin** and ¼ teaspoon **Ground Nutmeg** for Curry Powder, Ground Cumin, Paprika, Seasoned Salt and Ground Red Pepper. Prepare as directed.

Asian-Style Beef Ribs

PREP TIME: 10 minutes · MARINATE TIME: 30 minutes · COOK TIME: 1 hour

¾ cup orange juice concentrate
¼ cup soy sauce
1 tablespoon **Paprika**
2 teaspoons **Ground Ginger**
1 teaspoon **Ground Mustard**
1 teaspoon **Garlic Powder**
¼ teaspoon **Ground Red Pepper**
4 pounds beef short ribs

1 **MIX** orange juice concentrate, soy sauce, Paprika, Ground Ginger, Ground Mustard, Garlic Powder and Ground Red Pepper in large resealable bag. Seal and shake to mix. Add ribs, seal and knead to coat evenly. Refrigerate 30 minutes. Remove ribs from bag and place in 9x13-inch baking pan. Discard marinade.

2 **BAKE** in preheated 350°F oven 1 hour until cooked through. Serve hot.

▶ **MAKES 6 SERVINGS**

flavor variations

● **SLOW COOKER ASIAN-STYLE BEEF RIBS**
Place ribs in slow cooker. Mix remaining ingredients and pour over ribs. Cook on HIGH 4 hours or LOW 8 hours. (The ribs will not be crisp, but will still be delicious.)

● **GRILLED ASIAN-STYLE RIBS**
Marinate ribs as directed. Remove ribs from marinade and grill over medium-high heat, turning frequently, 10 minutes or until edges are dark brown and very crisp. Move ribs to edge of grill. Cover and grill 45 minutes or until meat is cooked through and tender.

Thai Beef Salad

PREP TIME: 15 minutes

1 pound sliced deli roast beef, cut into
  ½-inch strips
1 package (5 to 6 ounces) pre-washed
  baby spinach
1 medium red onion, peeled and thinly sliced
1 cup sliced radishes
Leaves from 1 small bunch fresh mint
¼ cup vegetable oil
Juice of 2 limes
1 teaspoon low-sodium soy sauce
1 teaspoon sugar
1 teaspoon **Chili Powder**
1 teaspoon **Cilantro Leaves**
½ teaspoon **Garlic Salt**
¼ teaspoon **Ground Red Pepper**

1 **TOSS** together beef, spinach, onion, radishes and mint leaves in large bowl.

2 **WHISK** oil, lime juice and soy sauce in small bowl until blended. Add sugar, Chili Powder, Cilantro Leaves, Garlic Salt and Ground Red Pepper and whisk until sugar is dissolved.

3 **POUR** dressing over beef mixture, tossing to coat evenly. Serve immediately.

► **MAKES 4 SERVINGS**

flavor variations

● **THAI CHICKEN SALAD**
Use 1 pound cooked sliced chicken breast in place of beef. Prepare as directed.

● **THAI BEEF SALAD WITH ARUGULA**
Use baby arugula in place of spinach. Prepare as directed.

● **THAI BASIL BEEF SALAD**
Substitute 1 teaspoon **Basil Leaves** for Cilantro Leaves. Prepare as directed.

Italian Sausages with Roasted Peppers and Onions

PREP TIME: 15 minutes · COOK TIME: 20 minutes

1½ pounds Italian sausage links, hot or mild
    or a combination of both
1 jar (8 ounces) Italian roasted peppers,
    drained and chopped
1 large onion, peeled and sliced
2 cans (14½ ounces <u>each</u>) chopped tomatoes
2 teaspoons **Italian Seasoning**
½ teaspoon **Garlic Powder**
½ teaspoon **Ground Black Pepper**

1 **COOK** sausages in large skillet over medium-high heat, turning occasionally, 5 minutes or until brown.

2 **ADD** peppers, onion, tomatoes, Italian Seasoning, Garlic Powder and Ground Black Pepper. Bring to a simmer; lower heat and cook 15 minutes or until sausages are cooked through.

► **MAKES 4 SERVINGS**

flavor variations

● **ITALIAN TURKEY SAUSAGES WITH ROASTED PEPPERS AND ONIONS**
Use 1½ pounds Italian turkey sausage for pork sausage. Prepare as directed.

● **ITALIAN TURKEY SAUSAGES WITH BELL PEPPERS AND ONIONS**
Omit jarred roasted peppers. Use 2 fresh red <u>or</u> green bell peppers, sliced. Prepare as directed.

● **ITALIAN SAUSAGES WITH SPICY PEPPERS AND ONIONS**
Add ½ teaspoon **Crushed Red Pepper** to tomato mixture.

● **SAUSAGE AND PEPPER HEROES**
Prepare as directed. Divide sausage mixture among 4 toasted Italian hero rolls.

Pork Chops with Mediterranean Flavor

PREP TIME: 15 minutes · **MARINATE TIME:** 2 hours · **COOK TIME:** 30 minutes

2 teaspoons **Seasoned Salt**
1 teaspoon **Thyme Leaves**
1⅓ teaspoon **Rubbed Sage**
1 teaspoon **Garlic Powder**
1 teaspoon **Coarse Ground Black Pepper**
4 center-cut pork chops (1 inch thick), trimmed of excess fat

1 MIX Seasoned Salt, Thyme Leaves, Rubbed Sage, Garlic Powder and Coarse Ground Black Pepper in small bowl. Rub mixture into both sides of each chop. Place chops in single layer in 9x13-inch baking dish and cover with plastic wrap. Refrigerate at least 2 hours or overnight.

2 GRILL over medium-high heat, 5 minutes on each side. Move to cooler part of grill and grill, turning occasionally, 20 minutes or until chops are cooked through.

▶ **MAKES 4 SERVINGS**

flavor variations

● **MEDITERRANEAN PORK TENDERLOIN**
Use 1 (1-pound) pork tenderloin in place of pork chops. Marinate as directed. Grill over medium-high heat 18 to 20 minutes or until cooked through. To serve, slice on the bias and serve hot. Prepare as directed.

● **PAN-GRILLED MEDITERRANEAN PORK CHOPS**
Prepare as directed. Heat grill pan over medium-high heat until hot. Cook pork chops 5 minutes per side. Reduce heat to medium, cover and cook 20 minutes or until cooked through. Prepare as directed.

● **PEPPER MEDLEY PORK CHOPS**
Substitute 1 teaspoon **Mixed Peppercorn Medley** for Coarse Ground Black Pepper. Prepare as directed.

Enchilada Pork Chops

PREP TIME: 10 minutes · COOK TIME: 30 minutes

2 tablespoons vegetable oil
4 boneless pork chops (¾ inch thick),
   trimmed of excess fat
1 cup chopped onion
1 can (14½ ounces) diced tomatoes
   with ½ cup juice
1 package **Enchilada Sauce Mix**
1 cup water

1 HEAT oil in large heavy skillet over high heat. Add chops and sear, turning frequently, 2 minutes on each side or until golden. Remove pan from heat and pour off excess fat.

2 STIR in onions and tomatoes and juice. Stir in Enchilada Sauce Mix and water. Cover, reduce heat to medium and simmer 25 minutes or until chops are cooked through.

► **MAKES 4 SERVINGS**

flavor variations

● **ENCHILADA CHICKEN**
Use 4 boneless chicken thighs in place of pork chops. Prepare as directed.

● **CHILI PORK CHOPS**
Substitute 1 package **Chili Seasoning Mix** for Enchilada Seasoning Mix. Prepare as directed.

Sesame-Curry Pork Tenderloin

PREP TIME: 10 minutes · COOK TIME: 20 minutes

½ cup low-sodium soy sauce
¼ cup honey
1 tablespoon **Curry Powder**
1 tablespoon **Sesame Seed**
⅛ teaspoon **Ground Red Pepper**
1½ pounds pork tenderloin

1 WHISK together soy sauce, honey, Curry Powder, Sesame Seed and Ground Red Pepper in small bowl. Generously brush tenderloin with mixture. Reserve remaining mixture. Place tenderloin in 9x13-inch baking dish.

2 BAKE in preheated 400°F oven 20 minutes, brushing meat with soy mixture, until an instant-read thermometer inserted into thickest part reads 155°F. Remove from oven and let rest 10 minutes before slicing.

▶ MAKES 4 SERVINGS

flavor variations

● SESAME-CURRY SALMON FILLETS
Coat flesh side of 4 salmon fillets with glaze. Place skin side down in baking dish. Prepare as directed.

● SESAME-SOY PORK TENDERLOIN
Substitute 1 teaspoon **Ground Ginger**, ½ teaspoon **Garlic Powder** and ½ teaspoon **Chives** for Curry Powder.

Spicy and Sweet Pulled Pork

PREP TIME: 20 minutes · COOK TIME: LOW, 8 hours; HIGH, 4 hours

1 boneless pork shoulder roast <u>or</u>
  Boston butt (4 pounds)
10 **Whole Cloves**
1 package **Slow Cookers BBQ
  Pulled Pork Seasoning**
2 tablespoons **Cinnamon Sugar**
1 large onion, chopped
½ cup tomato juice
1 cup water

Toasted crusty rolls, for serving (optional)

1 **RINSE** pork and pat dry. Stud meat with Whole Cloves. Place meat in slow cooker. Add Pulled Pork Seasoning, Cinnamon Sugar, onion, tomato juice, and water. Cover and cook on LOW 8 hours.

2 **REMOVE** pork from cooker; discard cloves. Using 2 forks, pull cooked meat into shreds.

3 **COMBINE** shredded pork with sauce that remains in slow cooker. Serve with toasted crusty rolls, if desired.

▶ **MAKES 12 SERVINGS**

flavor variations

● **PULLED PORK WITH PEPPERS**
Add 2 small chopped bell peppers to slow cooker. Prepare as directed.

● **APPLE-SPICE PULLED PORK**
Reduce Cinnamon Sugar to 1 tablespoon. Add 1 tablespoon **Apple Pie Spice** to slow cooker. Prepare as directed.

Sage and Onion Pork Roast

PREP TIME: 8 minutes · COOK TIME: 1 hour 30 minutes

2 teaspoons **Rubbed Sage**
1 teaspoon **Onion Powder**
1 teaspoon **Garlic Pepper**
½ teaspoon **Seasoned Salt**
2 tablespoons olive oil
1 (2-pound) boneless pork loin
1 package **Pork Gravy Mix**
1 cup water

1 **MIX** Rubbed Sage, Onion Powder, Garlic Pepper and Seasoned Salt in small bowl. Generously coat roast with olive oil, then sprinkle with Sage mixture. Place on rack in roasting pan.

2 **ROAST** in preheated 450°F oven 30 minutes. Reduce heat to 350°F and roast 1 hour or until instant-read thermometer inserted into thickest part reads 155°F. Remove from oven and let rest 10 minutes before slicing.

3 **MEANWHILE,** prepare gravy. Pour excess fat from pan and discard. Pour remaining juices into saucepan. Heat over medium heat and stir in Pork Gravy Mix and water. Simmer 1 minute or until thickened. Slice roast and spoon gravy over to serve.

► **MAKES 4 SERVINGS**

flavor variations

● THYME AND ONION PORK ROAST
Substitute 2 teaspoons **Thyme Leaves** for Rubbed Sage. Prepare as directed.

● SAGE AND ONION PORK ROAST WITH WHITE WINE GRAVY
Prepare roast as directed. To make gravy, use ½ cup white wine in place of ½ cup water.

Fish & Shellfish

Grilled Salmon Steaks

PREP TIME: 15 minutes · **COOK TIME:** 10 minutes

4 salmon steaks (6 ounces each)
4 teaspoons olive oil
2 tablespoons **Grill Mates® Montreal Chicken Seasoning**

1 **DRIZZLE** each salmon steak with 1 teaspoon olive oil and sprinkle with Chicken Seasoning.

2 **GRILL** salmon 5 minutes on each side or until cooked through. Serve hot.

► **MAKES 4 SERVINGS**

....

flavor variations

....

● **GRILLED MONTREAL SHRIMP**
Use 1½ pounds peeled and deveined jumbo shrimp in place of salmon. Thread shrimp onto skewers and grill 3 minutes per side or until cooked through.

● **MESQUITE GRILLED SALMON**
Substitute 2 tablespoons **Grill Mates® Mesquite Seasoning** for Chicken Seasoning. Prepare as directed.

Baked Catfish with Seasoned Breadcrumbs

PREP TIME: 5 minutes · **COOK TIME:** 10 minutes

4 catfish fillets
½ cup panko (Japanese breadcrumbs)
2 tablespoons **OLD BAY® Seasoning**
1 teaspoon **Parsley Flakes**
1 tablespoon vegetable oil

1 **PLACE** fillets in a single layer on foil-lined baking sheet. Mix panko, OLD BAY, Parsley Flakes and oil in small bowl. Sprinkle fish with panko mixture.

2 **BAKE** in preheated 375°F oven 10 minutes or until fish is firm to the touch and crust is golden brown.

▶ **MAKES 4 SERVINGS**

flavor variations

● **TRADITIONAL BREADED CATFISH**
Use regular breadcrumbs in place of panko. Prepare as directed.

● **BAKED LEMON PEPPER CATFISH**
Add ½ teaspoon **Lemon Pepper** to breadcrumb mixture. Prepare as directed.

● **BAKED CATFISH WITH HERBED BREADCRUMBS**
Substitute 1 tablespoon **Parsley Flakes,** 1 tablespoon **Italian Seasoning** and ¼ teaspoon **Celery Seed** for OLD BAY. Prepare as directed.

Spiced Tilapia

PREP TIME: 5 minutes · **COOK TIME:** 8 minutes

½ teaspoon **Chili Powder**
½ teaspoon **Paprika**
¼ teaspoon **Ground Cumin**
¼ teaspoon **Lemon Pepper**
¼ teaspoon **Seasoned Salt**
⅛ teaspoon **Onion Powder**
4 skinless, boneless tilapia fillets

1 **MIX** Chili Powder, Paprika, Ground Cumin, Lemon Pepper, Seasoned Salt and Onion Powder in small bowl. Spray tilapia with nonstick spray or brush with oil. Coat both sides of fish with seasoning. Place in single layer on broiler pan.

2 **BROIL** 6 to 8 minutes or until fish is firm to the touch and flakes easily when pierced with fork.

► **MAKES 4 SERVINGS**

flavor variations

● CURRIED TILAPIA
Substitute ½ teaspoon **Curry Powder**, ½ teaspoon **Pumpkin Pie Spice** and ⅛ teaspoon **Ground Red Pepper** for Ground Cumin, Lemon Pepper, Seasoned Salt and Onion Powder. Prepare as directed.

● GRILLED SPICED TILAPIA
Prepare as directed. Grill fillets over direct medium-high heat 3 minutes on each side or until cooked through.

Lemony Shrimp Skewers

PREP TIME: 10 minutes · **MARINATE TIME:** 30 minutes · **COOK TIME:** 6 minutes

⅓ cup olive oil
2 tablespoons lemon juice
1 tablespoon **OLD BAY® Seasoning**
1 teaspoon **Onion Powder**
2 pounds jumbo tail-on shrimp, peeled
   and deveined
2 medium red bell peppers, cut into
   1-inch squares
1 large zucchini, sliced ¼ inch thick
1 large lemon, sliced ¼ inch thick

1 **MIX** oil, lemon juice, OLD BAY and Onion Powder in large resealable bag. Add shrimp, seal and refrigerate 30 minutes. Remove shrimp from marinade and thread onto skewers, alternating with bell pepper pieces and zucchini and lemon slices. Discard marinade.

2 **GRILL** skewers over direct medium-high heat 3 minutes on each side or until shrimp are opaque and vegetables are golden and crisp-tender.

► **MAKES 4 SERVINGS**

· ·

flavor variations

· ·

● MONTREAL SHRIMP SKEWERS
Substitute 1 tablespoon **Grill Mates®**
Montreal Chicken Seasoning for OLD BAY
and Onion Powder. Prepare as directed.

● ITALIAN SHRIMP SKEWERS
Substitute 1 tablespoon **Italian Seasoning**
for OLD BAY and Onion Powder. Prepare as
directed.

Fish Enchiladas with Quick Ranchero Sauce

PREP TIME: 15 minutes · COOK TIME: 25 minutes

1 package **Enchilada Sauce Mix**
1 can (8 ounces) tomato sauce
1½ cups water
1 pound cooked boneless skinless tilapia,
    flaked (about 3 cups)
1 can (4 ounces) diced green chiles, drained
1 cup shredded pepper Jack cheese, divided
8 (6-inch) warm flour tortillas

1 **COOK** Enchilada Sauce Mix according to package directions, using tomato sauce and water for liquid. Spoon ½ cup sauce in bottom of 11x7-inch baking dish.

2 **MIX** fish with green chiles and ½ cup cheese. Spoon 1 tablespoon sauce on one tortilla. Top with ½ cup fish mixture. Roll up tortilla and place seam side down in baking dish. Repeat with remaining filling and tortillas. Top with remaining sauce and cheese.

3 **BAKE** in preheated 375°F oven 12 minutes or until sauce is bubbling and cheese has melted.

► **MAKES 4 SERVINGS**

flavor variations

● **CHICKEN RANCHERO ENCHILADAS**
Use 3 cups shredded cooked chicken in place of tilapia. Prepare as directed.

● **FISH ENCHILADAS WITH GARLICKY RANCHERO SAUCE**
Add ½ teaspoon **California Style® Wet Garlic** to filling. Prepare as directed.

● **FISH ENCHILADAS WITH TOMATILLO SAUCE**
Substitute 1 teaspoon **Ground Cumin**, ¼ teaspoon **Oregano Leaves** and ¼ teaspoon **Ground Red Pepper** for Enchilada Sauce Mix. Use 1 can (7 ounces) chopped green chiles, 1 jar tomatillo-based salsa and ½ cup vegetable broth in place of water and tomato sauce. Stir together. Prepare as directed.

OLD BAY® Shrimp Scampi

PREP TIME: 5 minutes · **COOK TIME:** 4 minutes

2 tablespoons olive oil
2 teaspoons **California Style® Wet Garlic**
1 pound large shrimp, peeled and
  deveined
1½ teaspoons **OLD BAY® Seasoning**
1 tablespoon lemon juice
1 teaspoon **Parsley Flakes**

1 **HEAT** oil in large skillet over medium heat. Add Wet Garlic; stir 30 seconds or just until fragrant. (Do not brown.)

2 **ADD** shrimp and OLD BAY. Cook, stirring, 3 to 4 minutes or until shrimp turn pink. Stir in lemon juice and Parsley Flakes. Serve immediately.

▶ **MAKES 4 SERVINGS**

flavor variations

● SPICY SHRIMP SCAMPI
Add ¼ teaspoon **Crushed Red Pepper** to Wet Garlic. Prepare as directed.

● SHRIMP SCAMPI WITH LINGUINE
Prepare shrimp as above. Cook 1 pound linguine according to package directions for al dente. Drain pasta and add to shrimp in pan. Toss to coat pasta and serve.

OLD BAY® Shrimp Grits

PREP TIME: 15 minutes · **COOK TIME:** 25 minutes

4 cups cooked grits
1 cup 2% milk
1 cup shredded low-fat Swiss or Fontina
  cheese
2 eggs, beaten
1½ teaspoons **OLD BAY® Seasoning**
1 pound cooked shrimp, chopped

1 **MIX** grits, milk, cheese, eggs and OLD BAY in medium bowl. Stir in shrimp. Pour mixture into lightly greased 2-quart casserole dish.

2 **BAKE** in preheated 375°F oven 25 minutes or until hot and bubbling.

► MAKES 4 SERVINGS

flavor variations

● CURRY SHRIMP GRITS
Substitute 1 teaspoon **Curry Powder**, ½ teaspoon **Pumpkin Pie Spice** and ⅛ teaspoon **Ground Red Pepper** for OLD BAY. Prepare as directed.

● SHRIMP AND HAM GRITS
Add 1 cup diced ham with the shrimp. Substitute 1 teaspoon **Season-All® Seasoned Salt**, ⅛ teaspoon **Ground Nutmeg** and ¼ teaspoon **Paprika** for OLD BAY. Prepare as directed.

● HERBED SHRIMP GRITS
Substitute ½ teaspoon **Thyme Leaves**, ½ teaspoon **Celery Salt**, ½ teaspoon **Basil Leaves**, ¼ teaspoon **Onion Powder**, ¼ teaspoon **Garlic Powder** and ½ teaspoon **Ground Black Pepper** for OLD BAY. Prepare as directed.

Shrimp and Tomato Pizza

PREP TIME: 15 minutes · **COOK TIME:** 25 minutes

1 (12-inch) pizza crust
1½ cups shredded Mozzarella cheese
1 cup diced tomatoes
½ pound large shrimp, peeled, deveined and
  cut in half, lengthwise
1½ teaspoons **Italian Seasoning**
½ teaspoon **Crushed Red Pepper**
  or to taste
3 tablespoons extra-virgin olive oil

1 **PLACE** pizza crust on pizza pan or stone. Top with even layers of Mozzarella, tomatoes and shrimp. Sprinkle with Italian Seasoning and Crushed Red Pepper. Drizzle with olive oil.

2 **BAKE** in preheated 425°F oven 20 to 25 minutes or until cheese is melted and shrimp is cooked through.

► **MAKES ONE 12-INCH PIZZA**

flavor variations

● **CHICKEN AND TOMATO PIZZA**
Use 1 cup diced cooked chicken in place of shrimp. Prepare as directed.

● **MAKE-YOUR-OWN PIZZA**
Add your favorite pizza toppings: ½ cup sliced green or black olives, 1 teaspoon **California Style® Wet Garlic** or ½ cup chopped red onions with tomatoes. Prepare as directed.

Pasta & Grains

Old Fashioned Macaroni and Cheese

PREP TIME: 15 minutes · COOK TIME: 20 minutes, plus pasta cooking time

1½ cups milk
1 teaspoon **Ground Mustard**
1 teaspoon **Paprika**
¼ cup butter
8 ounces elbow macaroni, cooked and
   drained
¾ pound sharp Cheddar cheese, grated
½ teaspoon **Onion Powder**
½ teaspoon salt
½ teaspoon **Coarse Ground Black Pepper**

1 STIR together milk, Ground Mustard and Paprika in medium bowl until blended. Set aside.

2 HEAT butter in medium saucepan over medium-low heat until melted. Stir in cooked macaroni, then stir in milk mixture, cheese, Onion Powder, salt and Coarse Ground Black Pepper.

3 COOK over low heat, stirring constantly, 10 minutes or until sauce barely begins to bubble around edges of pan. (**Do not boil.**) Reduce heat and cook, stirring, 5 minutes, just until sauce has thickened. Serve hot.

▶ **MAKES 4 SERVINGS**

· ·

flavor variations

· ·

● MAKE-YOUR-OWN MAC AND CHEESE
Use your favorite cheese or combination of cheeses in place of Cheddar. Just be sure not to boil the sauce; it will separate and the cheese will curdle. Prepare as directed.

● MAC AND CHEESE WITH PEAS AND HAM
Add ½ cup frozen peas to macaroni cooking water 1 minute before macaroni is cooked. Prepare as directed. Just before serving, stir in 1 cup diced ham.

● GARLICKY MACARONI AND CHEESE
Add ⅛ teaspoon **Garlic Powder** to milk mixture. Prepare as directed.

Turkey-Noodle Bake

PREP TIME: 20 minutes · **COOK TIME:** 30 minutes, plus pasta cooking time

1 bag (12 ounces) egg noodles, cooked and drained
8 ounces cooked turkey, diced
1 teaspoon **Poultry Seasoning**
½ teaspoon **Paprika**
1 package **Turkey Gravy Mix**
1 cup cold water
1 cup low-fat milk
½ cup grated Parmesan cheese, optional

1 **COMBINE** noodles, turkey, Poultry Seasoning and Paprika in lightly greased 2-quart casserole.

2 **STIR** Turkey Gravy Mix and water in a medium microwaveable bowl. Microwave on high for 2 minutes or until thickened. Stir in milk, then pour gravy mixture over noodle mixture. Stir to mix.

3 **BAKE** in preheated 375°F oven 20 minutes. Sprinkle with cheese, if desired, and bake 10 minutes longer or until sauce is bubbling and the top is golden.

▶ **MAKES 4 SERVINGS**

flavor variations

● **TURKEY-NOODLE BAKE WITH ONION**
Add 1 teaspoon **Minced Onion** to noodle mixture. Prepare as directed.

● **TURKEY-NOODLE BAKE WITH THYME**
Substitute ½ teaspoon **Thyme Leaves** for Paprika. Prepare as directed.

Angel Hair Pasta with Fresh Tomato Sauce

PREP TIME: 15 minutes · COOK TIME: 15 minutes

3 tablespoons extra-virgin olive oil
1½ pounds ripe tomatoes, cored and
   chopped
1 tablespoon **Basil Leaves**
½ teaspoon **Garlic Powder**
½ teaspoon **Oregano Leaves**
¼ teaspoon salt
½ teaspoon **Ground Black Pepper**
1 pound angel hair pasta

1 **HEAT** oil in large nonstick skillet over medium heat 1 minute. Remove pan from heat. Add tomatoes, Basil Leaves, Garlic Powder and Oregano Leaves. Season with salt and Ground Black Pepper and set aside while cooking pasta.

2 **COOK** angel hair pasta according to package directions for al dente. Remove from heat and drain well. Place in serving bowl. Add sauce, tossing to coat pasta. Serve immediately.

► MAKES 4 SERVINGS

flavor variations

● ANGEL HAIR PASTA WITH
   GARLICKY TOMATO SAUCE
Substitute 1 teaspoon **California Style® Wet Garlic** for Garlic Powder. Prepare as directed.

● ANGEL HAIR PASTA WITH
   EVEN QUICKER FRESH TOMATO SAUCE
Substitute 2 tablespoons **Italian Seasoning** for Basil Leaves, Garlic Powder and Oregano Leaves. Prepare as directed.

Bow Ties with Bacon and Asparagus

PREP TIME: 15 minutes · COOK TIME: 15 minutes, plus pasta cooking time

½ pound thick bacon, diced
½ pound asparagus ends trimmed and cut
  on the bias into 1-inch pieces
2 teaspoons **Italian Seasoning**
½ teaspoon **Crushed Red Pepper**
¼ teaspoon **Garlic Salt**
1 pound bow tie pasta, cooked and drained
½ cup grated pecorino Romano cheese

1 COOK bacon in large nonstick skillet over medium heat, stirring frequently, 6 minutes or until crisp. Stir in asparagus, Italian Seasoning, Crushed Red Pepper and Garlic Salt.

2 COOK, stirring occasionally, 5 minutes or until asparagus is crisp-tender. Remove pan from heat.

3 ADD bow ties to bacon mixture. Toss, top with cheese and serve.

► MAKES 4 SERVINGS

. . . .

flavor variations

. . . .

● BOW TIES WITH BACON, ASPARAGUS,
   BASIL AND TARRAGON
Substitute 1 teaspoon <u>each</u> **Basil Leaves**
and **Tarragon Leaves** for Italian Seasoning.

● BOW TIES WITH ASPARAGUS AND
   PARMESAN
Prepare as directed. Use ½ cup grated
Parmesan in place of pecorino Romano.

● BOW TIES WITH BACON AND BROCCOLI
Use ½ pound broccoli florets in place of
asparagus. Prepare as directed.

Pasta with Thai Peanut Sauce

PREP TIME: 15 minutes · **COOK TIME:** 5 minutes, plus pasta cooking time

1 cup creamy peanut butter
1 cup lite unsweetened coconut milk
⅓ cup rice wine vinegar
¼ cup soy sauce
2 tablespoons orange juice concentrate
1 teaspoon **Ground Ginger**
½ teaspoon **Crushed Red Pepper**
¼ teaspoon **Ground Cumin**
¼ teaspoon **Ground Allspice**
1 pound thin spaghetti, cooked and drained
1 tablespoon **Cilantro Leaves**

1 **WHISK** peanut butter, coconut milk, vinegar, soy sauce, orange juice concentrate, Ground Ginger, Crushed Red Pepper, Ground Cumin and Ground Allspice in medium saucepan until smooth. Cook over medium heat, stirring frequently, 5 minutes or just until mixture comes to a boil.

2 **POUR** sauce over hot spaghetti. Toss until spaghetti is coated. Sprinkle with Cilantro Leaves and serve.

► MAKES 4 SERVINGS

flavor variations

● **THAI NOODLES WITH CHICKEN**
Prepare as directed. Just before serving, stir in 2 cups cooked shredded chicken.

● **THAI NOODLES WITH BASIL**
Prepare as directed. Substitute 1 tablespoon **Basil Leaves** for Cilantro Leaves.

● **SESAME THAI NOODLES**
Prepare as directed. Sprinkle noodles with 1 tablespoon toasted **Sesame Seed** (see page 29) just before serving.

Singapore Noodles

PREP TIME: 15 minutes · **COOK TIME:** 5 minutes, plus pasta cooking time

½ cup lite unsweetened coconut milk
½ cup vegetable broth
3 tablespoons soy sauce
½ teaspoon **Curry Powder**
1 teaspoon honey
¼ teaspoon **Ground Cumin**
⅛ teaspoon **Ground Red Pepper**
½ pound angel hair pasta, cooked and drained
¼ cup chopped scallions (white and green parts)
½ cup diced red bell pepper
1 tablespoon toasted **Sesame Seed** (see page 29)

1 **STIR** coconut milk, vegetable broth, soy sauce, Curry Powder, honey, Ground Cumin and Ground Red Pepper in small saucepan over medium heat. Cook, stirring, 5 minutes or until sauce is hot.

2 **PLACE** hot pasta in serving bowl.

3 **ADD** sauce to pasta and toss to coat. Sprinkle with scallions, bell pepper and Sesame Seed. Serve hot.

► **MAKES 2 SERVINGS**

flavor variations

● **SINGAPORE NOODLES WITH CHICKEN**
Prepare as directed. Just before serving, add 1 cup diced cooked chicken to pasta.

● **SINGAPORE NOODLES WITH PORK**
Prepare as directed. Just before serving, add 1 cup diced cooked boneless pork to pasta.

Fried Rice

PREP TIME: 5 minutes · **COOK TIME:** 15 minutes

2 tablespoons soy sauce
½ teaspoon **Ground Ginger**
½ teaspoon **Garlic Powder**
1 teaspoon vegetable or sesame oil
1 cup vegetables (broccoli florets, thawed
    frozen diced carrots, thawed frozen peas,
    diced red bell pepper, etc.)
2 large eggs, beaten
2½ cups leftover cooked rice
⅓ cup chopped scallions with some green
    part included

1   **STIR** soy sauce, Ground Ginger and Garlic Powder in small bowl. Set aside.

2   **HEAT** oil in nonstick skillet or wok over high heat until nearly smoking. Add vegetables and stir-fry 7 minutes. Push to edge of wok. Add eggs to center of wok and cook until edges are set. Push eggs to edges of wok.

3   **ADD** rice and toss to heat through. Stir in soy sauce mixture, then add scallions. Remove from heat and serve.

▶ **MAKES 4 SERVINGS**

flavor variations

● **FRIED RICE WITH SESAME SEED**
Prepare as directed. Sprinkle rice with
1 tablespoon toasted **Sesame Seed**
(see page 29) before serving.

● **SPICY FRIED RICE**
Add ¼ teaspoon **Ground Red Pepper** to
soy sauce mixture. Prepare as directed.

● **CHICKEN FRIED RICE**
Prepare as directed. Add 1 cup diced cooked
boneless chicken to pan with rice.

● **4-STEP FRIED RICE**
Use freshly cooked rice in place of the
leftover rice. Add just before serving and
toss very gently so rice doesn't break.

Red Rice

PREP TIME: 5 minutes · COOK TIME: 10 minutes

1 can (28 ounces) diced tomatoes
1 teaspoon **Italian Seasoning**
½ teaspoon **Garlic Powder**
3½ cups cooked white rice
½ teaspoon salt
½ teaspoon **Coarse Ground Black Pepper**
1 tablespoon **Parsley Flakes**

1 **COMBINE** tomatoes, Italian Seasoning and Garlic Powder in large saucepan over medium heat. Bring to a boil.

2 **STIR** in rice and season with salt and Coarse Ground Black Pepper. Bring to boil. Lower heat to medium-low.

3 **COVER** and cook 8 minutes or until rice has absorbed tomato juices. Remove from heat, stir in Parsley Flakes, and serve.

► SERVES 4 TO 6

flavor variations

● LOUISIANA-STYLE RED RICE
Substitute ½ teaspoon **Celery Salt** for salt. Prepare as directed.

● GARLICKY RED RICE
Substitute 1 teaspoon **California Style®** **Wet Garlic** for Garlic Powder. Prepare as directed.

● RED RICE WITH SHRIMP
Prepare as directed. Stir in 1 pound cooked peeled and deveined shrimp into rice with Parsley Flakes.

Slow-Cooker Risotto

PREP TIME: 5 minutes · COOK TIME: Slow cooker, HIGH, 2 hours; LOW, 4 hours

3½ cups chicken broth
¼ cup dry white wine
1 tablespoon extra-virgin olive oil
1 tablespoon **Minced Onion**
¼ teaspoon **Garlic Powder**
1¼ cups Arborio or other short-grain
    white rice
½ teaspoon salt
½ cup grated Parmesan cheese
1 tablespoon **Parsley Flakes**

1 COMBINE broth, wine and oil in slow cooker. Add Minced Onion, Garlic Powder, rice and salt. Stir to mix.

2 COVER and cook on HIGH 2 hours or LOW 4 hours. Just before serving, stir in cheese and Parsley Flakes.

► SERVES 4

flavor variations

● BAKED RISOTTO
Combine ingredients in 2-quart casserole dish. Cover and bake in preheated 350°F oven 45 minutes to 1 hour or until rice is tender and all moisture has been absorbed.

● RISOTTO WITH OLIVES
Prepare as directed. Add ½ cup sliced black olives with cheese and Parsley Flakes.

● RISOTTO WITH HERBS
Add 1 teaspoon **Italian Seasoning** with Minced Onion. Prepare as directed.

Orange-Spice Couscous

PREP TIME: 3 minutes · COOK TIME: 10 minutes

1½ cups chicken broth
½ cup orange juice
2 **Whole Cloves**
½ teaspoon salt
¼ teaspoon **Pumpkin Pie Spice**
1½ cups plain couscous
¼ cup chopped dried apricots (about 6)
2 tablespoons slivered almonds

1 **COMBINE** broth, juice, Whole Cloves, salt and Pumpkin Pie Spice in medium saucepan over medium heat. Bring to a boil. Immediately stir in couscous. Cover and remove from heat. Let stand 5 minutes.

2 **UNCOVER** and fluff with fork. Remove cloves and discard. Stir in apricots and almonds and serve.

► MAKES 6 SERVINGS

flavor variations

● VEGETARIAN ORANGE-SPICE COUSCOUS
Use 1½ cups vegetable broth in place of chicken broth. Prepare as directed.

● ORANGE-SPICE COUSCOUS
   WITH SCALLIONS
Stir in 2 tablespoons chopped scallions to broth mixture. Prepare as directed.

● ORANGE-GINGER COUSCOUS
Substitute ¼ teaspoon **Apple Pie Spice** for Pumpkin Pie Spice. Prepare as directed.

Parmesan Polenta

PREP TIME: 5 minutes · **COOK TIME:** 50 minutes

1 cup 2% milk (to replace 1 cup of water
   called for in package directions)
Water as directed on package (minus 1 cup)
1 teaspoon salt
2 cups quick-cooking polenta
1 teaspoon **Italian Seasoning**
½ teaspoon **Onion Powder**
½ cup grated Parmesan cheese
½ teaspoon **Coarse Ground Black Pepper**

1   **HEAT** milk, water and salt in large saucepan over high heat. Bring to boil and stir in polenta, Italian Seasoning, and Onion Powder. Bring to boil. Reduce heat and cook, stirring constantly, for 5 minutes or until mixture is thick. Remove from heat and stir in cheese and Coarse Ground Black Pepper. Spread evenly into 9x13-inch baking dish.

2   **BAKE** in preheated 350°F oven 40 to 45 minutes or until firm. Cut into wedges and serve.

► **MAKES 4 SERVINGS**

flavor variations

● **QUICK TOMATO-BASIL SALAD**
Toss 1 pint cherry or grape tomatoes with 1 teaspoon olive oil, 1 teaspoon **Basil Leaves** and ⅛ teaspoon salt.

● **PARMESAN POLENTA WITH MARINARA**
Prepare as directed. Top each serving with ½ cup warm marinara sauce.

● **PARMESAN POLENTA WITH BASIL
   AND OREGANO**
Substitute ½ teaspoon <u>each</u> **Basil Leaves** <u>and</u> **Oregano Leaves** for Italian Seasoning. Prepare as directed.

Slow-Cooker Barley Stew

PREP TIME: 15 minutes · **COOK TIME:** Slow cooker, HIGH, 3 hours; LOW, 6 hours

1 cup barley
2 medium potatoes, cubed
2 medium carrots, peeled, trimmed and diced
1 cup sliced button mushrooms
½ cup chopped onion
2 cans (14 ounces <u>each</u>) beef broth
1 package **Brown Gravy Mix**
1 tablespoon **Parsley Flakes**
¼ teaspoon **Ground Black Pepper**
4 cups water

1 **COMBINE** barley, potatoes, carrots, mushrooms, onion and broth in slow cooker. Add Brown Gravy Mix, Parsley Flakes, Ground Black Pepper and water. Cover and cook on HIGH 3 hours or LOW 6 hours. Serve hot.

▶ **MAKES 4 SERVINGS**

······································

flavor variations

······································

● MUSHROOM-BARLEY STEW
Use 4 cups chopped mushrooms in place of potatoes and carrots. Increase chopped onion by ½ cup and add ½ teaspoon **Thyme Leaves**. Prepare as directed.

● VEGETABLE-BARLEY STEW
Add ½ cup chopped celery, 1 large diced red bell pepper and ¼ teaspoon **Celery Seed** with potatoes and carrots. Prepare as directed.

Vegetables

Mediterranean Vegetable Sauté

PREP TIME: 15 minutes · **COOK TIME:** 20 minutes

¼ cup olive oil
1 pound eggplant, cut into cubes
1 large green bell pepper, diced
1 can (14½ ounces) diced tomatoes
1 cup diced red onions
½ cup chopped green olives
1 teaspoon **Garlic Salt**
½ teaspoon **Basil Leaves**
½ teaspoon **Oregano Leaves**
½ cup red wine vinegar
2 tablespoons light brown sugar
½ cup pine nuts

1 **HEAT** oil in large nonstick skillet over medium heat. Add eggplant and cook, stirring, 10 minutes or just until eggplant softens. Stir in bell pepper, tomatoes, onions, olives, Garlic Salt, Basil Leaves and Oregano Leaves.

2 **COOK** 5 minutes or just until vegetables have softened a bit. Stir in vinegar, sugar and pine nuts. Bring to a boil. Remove from heat and allow to cool. Serve at room temperature. (Although this dish can be eaten immediately, it is even better the next day. Cover and refrigerate overnight. Bring to room temperature before serving.)

▶ **MAKES 4 SERVINGS**

flavor variations

● **VEGETABLE SAUTÉ WITH ZUCCHINI**
Prepare as directed. Add 1 large chopped zucchini with bell pepper.

● **ITALIAN VEGETABLE SAUTÉ**
Substitute 2½ teaspoons **Italian Seasoning** for Garlic Salt, Basil Leaves and Oregano Leaves.

● **CAPONATA BRUSCHETTA**
Slice 1 loaf French bread into 32 (½-inch-thick) slices. Lightly brush both sides of each slice with olive oil. Bake in preheated 425°F oven 6 to 8 minutes or until lightly browned and crisp, turning once halfway through cooking. Cool on wire rack. If not using immediately, store cooled toasts in airtight container. To serve, top each toast with 1 tablespoon Mediterranean Vegetable Sauté.

Garlicky Broccoli

PREP TIME: 5 minutes · **COOK TIME:** 6 minutes

1 pound broccoli florets
½ teaspoon **Crushed Red Pepper**
1 tablespoon water
1 teaspoon **Onion Powder**
1 teaspoon **Garlic Salt**
1 tablespoon olive oil

Grated Parmesan cheese, for serving
(optional)

1 **COMBINE** broccoli and Crushed Red Pepper in microwave-proof bowl. Add water, cover bowl with plastic and cook on HIGH 1 minute or until bright green. Toss broccoli with Onion Powder and Garlic Salt.

2 **HEAT** oil in large nonstick skillet over high heat. Add broccoli mixture and cook, tossing, 5 minutes or until broccoli is slightly golden, but still crisp-tender. Sprinkle with cheese, if desired. Serve hot.

▸ **MAKES 4 SERVINGS**

flavor variations

● **GARLICKY BROCCOLI WITH SESAME SEED**
Add ½ teaspoon **Sesame Seed** with Garlic Salt and Onion Powder.

● **BROCCOLI SUPREME**
Substitute 2 teaspoons **Salad Supreme**® **Seasoning** for Crushed Red Pepper, Onion Powder and Garlic Salt.

Roasted Mixed Vegetables

PREP TIME: 15 minutes · COOK TIME: 15 minutes

1 pound asparagus, trimmed
3 portobello mushroom caps, cleaned
  and quartered
2 red bell peppers, cut into wedges
1 medium eggplant, cut into ½-inch thick
  slices, halved
¾ cup olive oil
½ cup balsamic vinegar
2 teaspoons **Thyme Leaves**
2 teaspoons **Rosemary Leaves**
2 teaspoons **Basil Leaves**
1 teaspoon **Pepper Medley Grinder**
1 teaspoon salt

1 **PLACE** asparagus, mushrooms, bell peppers and eggplant in a large rimmed baking pan. Add olive oil, vinegar, Thyme Leaves, Rosemary Leaves, Basil Leaves, Pepper Medley Grinder and salt, tossing to coat well.

2 **ROAST** in preheated 450°F oven 15 minutes or until vegetables are browned and tender.

► **MAKES 4 SERVINGS**

flavor variations

● **ROASTED MIXED VEGETABLES WITH
   BALSAMIC VINAIGRETTE**
Prepare as directed. Toss with 1 recipe Balsamic Vinaigrette (page 45). Serve warm.

● **ITALIAN ROASTED MIXED VEGETABLES**
Substitute 4 teaspoons **Italian Seasoning** for Thyme Leaves, Rosemary Leaves and Basil Leaves.

Pan-Roasted Cauliflower with Penne

PREP TIME: 10 minutes · COOK TIME: 13 minutes

3 tablespoons olive oil
1 medium head cauliflower, broken into small florets (about 4 cups)
1 tablespoon **Grill Mates® Spicy Montreal Steak Seasoning**
½ teaspoon **California Style® Wet Garlic**
1 pound penne pasta
½ teaspoon salt
¼ cup grated Parmesan cheese

1 **HEAT** oil in large nonstick skillet over medium heat. Add cauliflower, Steak Seasoning and Wet Garlic. Cook, stirring occasionally, about 10 minutes or until cauliflower is golden brown and cooked through.

2 **MEANWHILE** cook pasta according to package directions for al dente. Reserve 1 cup cooking water, then drain pasta. Stir drained pasta into cauliflower and add reserved cooking water. Cook, stirring, 3 minutes. Taste and season with salt. Pour into serving bowl, sprinkle with cheese and serve.

► **MAKES 4 SERVINGS**

flavor variations

● PENNE WITH CAULIFLOWER AND TUNA
Prepare as directed. Add 1 can tuna in olive oil, drained, to penne just before serving.

● ITALIAN PENNE WITH CAULIFLOWER
Substitute 1 tablespoon **Italian Seasoning** for Spicy Montreal Steak Seasoning. Prepare as directed.

Broiled Tomatoes

PREP TIME: 10 minutes · COOK TIME: 4 minutes

2 tablespoons breadcrumbs
1 tablespoon grated Parmesan cheese
1 teaspoon **Italian Seasoning**
½ teaspoon **Seasoned Salt**
4 ripe tomatoes, cored and cut in half, crosswise
4 teaspoons olive oil

1 **MIX** breadcrumbs, cheese, Italian Seasoning and Seasoned Salt in small bowl.

2 **SPRINKLE** cut side of each tomato with breadcrumb mixture (you will use about 1½ teaspoons on each). Drizzle each with ½ teaspoon olive oil and place cut side up on foil-lined broiler pan.

3 **BROIL** under preheated broiler 4 minutes or until tomatoes are hot and topping is brown and bubbly.

► MAKES 4 SERVINGS

flavor variations

● BROILED GREEN TOMATOES
Use green tomatoes in place of red and yellow tomatoes. Prepare as directed.

● SPICY BROILED TOMATOES
Add ¼ teaspoon **Crushed Red Pepper** to breadcrumb mixture. Prepare as directed.

● BROILED TOMATOES WITH THYME
Substitute 1 teaspoon **Thyme Leaves** for Italian Seasoning. Prepare as directed.

Pizza with Spinach, Garlic and Feta

PREP TIME: 10 minutes · COOK TIME: 10 minutes

4 cups baby spinach leaves
1 tablespoon extra-virgin olive oil
¾ teaspoons **Italian Seasoning**
¼ teaspoon **Lemon Pepper**
⅛ teaspoon **Garlic Powder**
1 (12-inch) pizza crust
8 ounces Feta crumbles

Balsamic Syrup (recipe follows), for serving,
   optional

1 **TOSS** spinach with olive oil. Sprinkle with Italian Seasoning, Lemon Pepper and Garlic Powder and toss. Pile spinach mixture on top of pizza crust. Sprinkle with Feta cheese.

2 **BAKE** in preheated 450°F oven 10 minutes or until spinach has wilted and cheese has melted. Remove from oven and drizzle with Balsamic Syrup, if desired.

► MAKES 4 SERVINGS

flavor variations

● **PIZZA WITH SPINACH, GARLIC AND GOAT CHEESE**
Prepare as directed. Use 1 cup crumbled goat cheese in place of Feta cheese.

● **PIZZA WITH MUSHROOMS AND FETA**
Use 4 cups sliced baby Bella mushrooms in place of spinach and 1 teaspoon **Thyme Leaves** for Italian Seasoning and Lemon Pepper. Heat oil in large nonstick skillet over medium-high heat. Add mushrooms and cook until wilted and most of the liquid has evaporated, 10 minutes. Stir in Thyme Leaves and Garlic Powder. Prepare as directed.

● **BALSAMIC SYRUP**
Bring 4 tablespoons balsamic vinegar to a boil. Cook until liquid becomes thick and syrupy. Use sparingly—the flavor is intense.

Butternut Squash Soup

PREP TIME: 5 minutes · COOK TIME: 15 minutes

2 packages (12 ounces <u>each</u>) frozen squash purée, thawed
2 to 3 tablespoons honey
¼ teaspoon **Ground Nutmeg**
¼ teaspoon **Ground Cinnamon**
¼ teaspoon **Ground Ginger**
¼ teaspoon **Ground Allspice**
1 can (14 ounces) chicken broth or vegetable broth
½ teaspoon <u>each</u> salt <u>and</u> **Ground White Pepper**
Chives, for garnish, optional

1 **MIX** squash, 2 tablespoons honey, Ground Nutmeg, Ground Cinnamon, Ground Ginger and Ground Allspice in medium saucepan. Stir in broth and season with salt and Ground White Pepper.

2 **HEAT** over medium heat; bring to a simmer. Simmer for 5 minutes or until the soup is hot and the flavors have blended. Taste and, if necessary, add more honey to reach desired sweetness. Serve sprinkled with Chives, if desired.

➤ **MAKES 6 SERVINGS**

flavor variations

● AUTUMN SQUASH SOUP
Substitute 2 teaspoons **Pumpkin Pie Spice** for Ground Nutmeg, Ground Cinnamon, Ground Ginger and Ground Allspice. Prepare as directed.

● SQUASH SOUP WITH SOUR CREAM
Prepare as directed. Top each serving with a dollop of sour cream.

● SQUASH SOUP WITH RAVIOLI
Prepare as directed. Cook 1 package fresh 3-cheese ravioli according to package directions and float a few cooked ravioli in each serving.

● INDIAN-SPICED SQUASH SOUP
Substitute 1 teaspoon **Curry Powder,** ½ teaspoon **Ground Cumin** and ½ teaspoon **Garlic Powder** for Ground Nutmeg, Ground Cinnamon, Ground Ginger and Ground Allspice. Prepare as directed.

Quick Corn Chowder

PREP TIME: 15 minutes · COOK TIME: 25 minutes

2 packages (10 ounces <u>each</u>) frozen corn
   kernels, thawed
2 cups frozen diced potatoes
1 cup chopped onion
1 small red bell pepper, diced
2 cups milk
2 cups chicken broth
¾ pound smoked ham, diced
1½ teaspoons **OLD BAY®️ Seasoning**
Pinch **Crushed Red Pepper**

1 **STIR** together corn, potatoes, onions and bell pepper in large saucepan. Add milk and broth and bring to a simmer over medium heat. Add ham, OLD BAY and Crushed Red Pepper.

2 **SIMMER** 15 minutes or until flavors are well-blended and vegetables are soft. Serve hot.

▶ **MAKES 4 SERVINGS**

flavor variations

● QUICK CORN AND SMOKED
   TURKEY CHOWDER
Use ¾ pound diced smoked turkey in place of smoked ham. Prepare as directed.

● INDIAN-SPICED QUICK CORN CHOWDER
Substitute 1 teaspoon **Curry Powder,**
¼ teaspoon **Ground Cumin** and ⅓ teaspoon **Ground Turmeric** for OLD BAY. Prepare as directed.

● EXTRA-THICK QUICK CORN CHOWDER
Prepare as directed. Transfer 1 cup cooked soup to blender. Puree until nearly smooth and stir into cooked soup.

Eggs

Breakfast Tacos

PREP TIME: 5 minutes · **COOK TIME:** 6 minutes

8 large eggs, beaten
1 can (16 ounces) refried beans, divided
½ teaspoon **Garlic Salt**
1 teaspoon canola oil
½ cup chopped scallions
½ teaspoon **Chili Powder**
8 taco shells, warmed
1 cup shredded Cheddar cheese

Prepared salsa for serving, optional

1 **BEAT** eggs in medium mixing bowl. Set aside. Mix refried beans and Garlic Salt in medium saucepan. Heat on low heat while preparing eggs.

2 **HEAT** oil in nonstick frying pan over medium heat. Add eggs to pan and cook, stirring frequently to scramble, 6 minutes or until eggs are cooked, but still moist. Remove from heat. Stir in scallions and Chili Powder.

3 **SPOON** 2 tablespoons beans into <u>each</u> taco shell. Divide eggs evenly among taco shells. Sprinkle with cheese and serve immediately with salsa, if desired.

► **MAKES 4 SERVINGS**

· ·
flavor variations
· ·

● **LOW-FAT BREAKFAST TACOS**
Use fat-free refried beans and 2 cups egg substitute in place of beans and eggs. Prepare as directed.

● **BREAKFAST TACOS WITH CILANTRO**
Add 1 teaspoon **Cilantro Leaves** to eggs before scrambling them. Prepare as directed.

Huevos Rancheros

PREP TIME: 10 minutes · COOK TIME: 5 minutes

2 tablespoons canola oil
8 large eggs
1 teaspoon **Chili Powder**
½ teaspoon **Garlic Salt**
4 warm corn tortillas
1 cup prepared salsa
⅓ cup crumbled Feta cheese
2 teaspoons **Cilantro Leaves**

1 **HEAT** oil in large nonstick skillet over medium heat. Break eggs into pan, cover and cook 4 minutes or until whites are set, but yolks are still runny. Season with Chili Powder and Garlic Salt. Remove from heat.

2 **PLACE** tortilla on each plate, top with salsa, add egg. Sprinkle with cheese and Cilantro Leaves.

► MAKES 4 SERVINGS

flavor variations

● HUEVOS RANCHEROS
WITH REFRIED BEANS
Prepare as directed. Cook 1 cup refried beans with ¼ teaspoon **Garlic Powder** and ¼ teaspoon **Ground Cumin**. Spread each tortilla with ¼ cup beans, then top with eggs, cheese and salsa.

● HUEVOS RANCHEROS
WITH MONTEREY JACK
Use ⅓ cup shredded Monterey Jack cheese in place of Feta. Prepare as directed.

Spanish Potato Omelet

PREP TIME: 10 minutes · **COOK TIME:** 30 minutes

2 tablespoons olive oil
2 cups frozen or refrigerated diced potatoes
½ cup diced red or green bell pepper
1 teaspoon **Garlic Powder**
½ teaspoon **Onion Powder**
8 large eggs, beaten
1 teaspoon salt
½ teaspoon **Ground Black Pepper**
2 teaspoons **Parsley Flakes**

1 **HEAT** oil in large nonstick frying pan over medium heat. Add potatoes, green pepper, Garlic Powder and Onion Powder and stir to combine. Reduce heat, cover and cook, stirring occasionally, 10 minutes or until potatoes are golden.

2 **STIR** together eggs, salt, Ground Black Pepper and Parsley Flakes in medium bowl. Pour mixture over potatoes. Smooth the top to make an even layer. Cover and cook on low about 15 minutes or until set in the center. Let stand 5 minutes before cutting into wedges.

➤ **MAKES 4 SERVINGS**

flavor variations

● SPANISH POTATO OMELET
   WITH GARLIC AND ONION
Add 1 medium diced onion <u>and</u> ½ teaspoon **California Style® Wet Garlic** with bell pepper. Prepare as directed.

● SPANISH POTATO OMELET WITH BASIL
Stir 1 teaspoon **Basil Leaves** into eggs. Prepare as directed.

● SPICY SPANISH POTATO OMELET
Stir ½ teaspoon **Crushed Red Pepper** into eggs. Prepare as directed.

Ricotta-Thyme Frittata

PREP TIME: 5 minutes · **COOK TIME:** 12 minutes

5 large eggs, beaten
¾ cup ricotta cheese, drained well
½ teaspoon **Thyme Leaves**
½ teaspoon **Garlic Powder**
¼ teaspoon **Ground Black Pepper**
½ medium bell pepper, diced
3 strips bacon, cooked crisp and crumbled
1 tablespoon olive oil

1 **STIR** eggs, cheese, Thyme Leaves, Garlic Powder, Ground Black Pepper, bell pepper and bacon until blended, set aside.

2 **HEAT** oil in large nonstick skillet over medium heat. Pour in egg mixture and cook without stirring 12 minutes or until eggs are set on top and the bottom is golden brown.

► **MAKES 4 TO 6 SERVINGS**

flavor variations

● **VEGETABLE FRITTATA**
Add 1 cup chopped cooked vegetables, such as broccoli, asparagus, onions, or cauliflower to egg mixture. Prepare as directed.

● **RICOTTA-DILL FRITTATA**
Substitute ½ teaspoon **Dill Weed** for Thyme Leaves. Prepare as directed.

● **FRITTATA WITH PARMESAN**
Prepare as directed. Sprinkle cooked frittata with 1 tablespoon grated Parmesan cheese. Broil 2 minutes or until cheese is golden.

Tomato Quiche

PREP TIME: 10 minutes · **COOK TIME:** 50 minutes

3 large tomatoes, chopped
1 tablespoon **Minced Onion**
1 teaspoon **Italian Seasoning**
¼ teaspoon **Garlic Powder**
3 large eggs
1½ cups half and half or heavy cream
¾ cup grated Parmesan cheese
½ teaspoon <u>each</u> salt <u>and</u> **Ground Black Pepper**
1 (9-inch) prepared pie shell

1 **COMBINE** tomatoes, Minced Onion, Italian Seasoning and Garlic Powder. Stir in eggs, half and half, cheese, salt and Ground Black Pepper. Pour mixture into pie shell.

2 **BAKE** in preheated 375°F oven for 45 to 50 minutes or until top is golden and quiche is set in the center. Remove from oven and let rest for 5 minutes before cutting into wedges and serving.

► **MAKES 4 SERVINGS**

flavor variations

● **TOMATO QUICHE WITH BASIL AND THYME** Substitute 1 teaspoon **Basil Leaves** <u>and</u> 1 teaspoon **Thyme Leaves** for Italian Seasoning. Prepare as directed.

● **ALL-SEASON TOMATO QUICHE** Use 2 cups well-drained canned diced tomatoes in place of fresh tomatoes. Prepare as directed.

Spiced Cheese Strata

PREP TIME: 15 minutes · COOK TIME: 1 hour 5 minutes

1 tablespoon melted butter
1 tablespoon canola oil
12 slices stale white bread, crusts removed, cut into small cubes
1½ cups grated Swiss cheese
8 large eggs
3 cups milk
1 tablespoon **Minced Onion**
2 teaspoons **Ground Mustard**
2 teaspoons Worcestershire sauce
½ teaspoon **Garlic Powder**
½ teaspoon **Paprika**
½ teaspoon <u>each</u> salt <u>and</u> **Ground Black Pepper**

1 **MIX** butter and oil in medium bowl. Add bread cubes and toss. Let stand until bread absorbs butter mixture. Place one-third of bread cubes in bottom of lightly greased 9x13-inch casserole. Sprinkle with half of cheese. Cover with half of remaining bread cubes, top with cheese and remaining bread cubes.

2 **WHISK** eggs, milk, Minced Onion, Ground Mustard, Worcestershire sauce, Garlic Powder, Paprika, salt and Ground Black Pepper in medium bowl. Pour over bread and cheese.

3 **BAKE** in preheated 350°F oven 1 hour 5 minutes or until bubbling and golden brown. Serve immediately.

▶ **MAKES 8 SERVINGS**

flavor variations

● **SPICED CHEDDAR OR JACK STRATA**
Use 1½ cups Cheddar or Monterey Jack cheese in place of Swiss cheese. Prepare as directed.

● **SPICED HAM AND CHEESE STRATA**
Mix 1 cup diced cooked ham with cheese. Prepare as directed.

● **SPICED CHEESE STRATA WITH THYME**
Add ½ teaspoon **Thyme Leaves** to egg mixture. Prepare as directed.

Raisin Bread Pudding

PREP TIME: 15 minutes · **COOK TIME:** 1 hour

4 large eggs
2 cups 2% milk
½ cup maple syrup
2 teaspoons **Apple Pie Spice**
12 slices raisin bread
8 ounces cream cheese, cut into ½-inch
   cubes

1 MIX eggs, milk, maple syrup and Apple Pie Spice in medium bowl. Set aside.

2 MAKE even layer of bread in bottom of lightly buttered 2½-quart casserole dish. Top with half of cheese cubes, another layer of bread and remaining cheese cubes. Cover with a third layer of bread. Pour egg mixture over bread.

3 BAKE in preheated 350°F oven 1 hour or until bubbling and golden brown.

▶ **MAKES 6 SERVINGS**

flavor variations

● **CINNAMON BREAD PUDDING**
Use cinnamon bread in place of raisin bread. Substitute 2 teaspoons **Ground Cinnamon** for Apple Pie Spice. Prepare as directed.

● **RAISIN-APPLE BREAD PUDDING**
Add 1 cup diced apples to egg mixture. Prepare as directed.

● **VANILLA RAISIN BREAD PUDDING**
Add 1 teaspoon **Pure Vanilla Extract** to egg mixture. Prepare as directed.

● **MAKE-AHEAD BREAD PUDDING**
Assemble pudding the day before. Cover with aluminum foil, and refrigerate overnight and up to 24 hours. Bake as directed.

Stuffed Peach French Toast

PREP TIME: 15 minutes · COOK TIME: 10 minutes

1 loaf (1 pound) egg bread, ends cut off and
  loaf sliced into 8 (1-inch thick) slices
8 ounces cream cheese, softened
½ cup peach preserves
½ cup chopped peaches
2 tablespoons powdered sugar, plus some
  for dusting
5 eggs
2 cups milk
2 tablespoons orange juice concentrate
2 teaspoons **Ground Cinnamon**
2 tablespoons light brown sugar

1 **CUT** each slice of bread from top to middle, forming a pocket. Do not cut through to bottom. Mix cream cheese, preserves, peaches and sugar. Fill each pocket with 2 tablespoons cheese mixture.

2 **WHISK** eggs, milk, orange juice concentrate, Ground Cinnamon and brown sugar in 9x13-inch baking dish until blended. Soak filled bread 10 minutes, turning once to coat both sides. The bread should be moist but not soggy.

3 **SPRAY** nonstick griddle with nonstick vegetable spray. Cook bread, turning once, 8 to 10 minutes or until bread is golden brown and cheese is hot and melting. Dust with powdered sugar and serve.

► **MAKES 4 SERVINGS**

flavor variations

● SPICED STUFFED FRENCH TOAST
Substitute 2 teaspoons **Apple Pie Spice** for Ground Cinnamon. Prepare as directed.

● STUFFED BLUEBERRY FRENCH TOAST
Use ½ cup blueberry preserves in place of peach preserves. Use ½ cup blueberries in place of chopped peaches. Prepare as directed.

● STUFFED PEACH-VANILLA FRENCH TOAST
Substitute ½ teaspoon **Pure Vanilla Extract** in place of orange juice concentrate. Prepare as directed.

Desserts

Spiced Carrot Cupcakes

PREP TIME: 25 minutes · COOK TIME: 25 minutes

1½ cups flour
½ teaspoon salt
1 teaspoon baking soda
1½ teaspoons **Pumpkin Pie Spice**
½ cup chopped walnuts
½ cup golden raisins
2 eggs
¾ cup brown sugar
1 teaspoon **Pure Vanilla Extract**
¾ cup vegetable oil
2 cups shredded carrots
  (3 to 4 medium carrots)

1 **MIX** flour, salt, baking soda, Pumpkin Pie Spice, walnuts and golden raisins in medium bowl. Set aside.

2 **BEAT** eggs, brown sugar and Pure Vanilla Extract with electric mixer on high until smooth. With mixer running, add oil. Fold in flour mixture and carrots. Scoop mixture into cups of muffin pan lined with paper liners, filling each cup ¾ full.

3 **BAKE** in 350°F preheated oven 25 minutes or until golden and top springs back when lightly pressed with fingertips. Cool completely on rack. Frost if desired.

► **MAKES 12 CUPCAKES**

· ·

flavor variations

· ·

● **QUICK CREAM CHEESE FROSTING**
Beat 8 ounces softened cream cheese, 2 tablespoons butter and ½ teaspoon **Pure Vanilla Extract** with electric mixer on medium speed until fluffy. Gradually whisk in 1½ cups sifted confectioner's sugar until the frosting reaches spreading consistency. Refrigerate until using.

● **CARROT-CINNAMON CUPCAKES**
Substitute 1 teaspoon **Ground Cinnamon** and ¼ teaspoon **Ground Nutmeg** for Pumpkin Pie Spice. Prepare as directed.

● **CARROT-ORANGE CUPCAKES**
Substitute ½ teaspoon **Orange Extract** for Pure Vanilla Extract. Add 1 tablespoon grated orange zest with the carrots. Prepare as directed.

Spiced Apple Bundt Cake

PREP TIME: 5 minutes · COOK TIME: 1 hour

3 cups all-purpose flour
1 teaspoon baking soda
1 tablespoon **Ground Cinnamon**
½ teaspoon **Ground Nutmeg**
½ teaspoon salt
3 large eggs
1¼ cups granulated sugar
½ cup light brown sugar
1½ cups canola oil
1 teaspoon **Pure Vanilla Extract**
2 sweet apples, such as Fuji or Gala, peeled,
   cored and chopped
1 tart apple (such as Granny Smith), peeled,
   cored and chopped
1 cup pecan pieces
½ cup raisins, optional

1 SIFT flour, baking soda, Ground Cinnamon, Ground Nutmeg and salt into small bowl. Set aside.

2 BEAT eggs and sugars with electric mixer on medium speed until blended. Stir in oil and Pure Vanilla Extract. Stir in dry ingredients, then fold in apples, pecans and raisins. Pour batter into lightly greased 12-cup Bundt pan.

3 BAKE in preheated 350°F oven 1 hour or until toothpick inserted near the center comes out clean. Invert the pan onto a wire rack and remove. Let cake cool at least 30 minutes before cutting.

► **MAKES 16 SERVINGS**

flavor variations

● **APPLE-SPICE CAKE**
Substitute 1 tablespoon plus ½ teaspoon **Apple Pie Spice** for Ground Cinnamon and Ground Nutmeg. Prepare as directed.

● **APPLE-CRANBERRY SPICE CAKE**
Use ½ cup dried cranberries in place of raisins. Prepare as directed.

● **APPLE-WALNUT SPICE CAKE**
Use 1 cup walnut pieces in place of pecans. Prepare as directed.

Vanilla Pound Cake

PREP TIME: 15 minutes · **COOK TIME:** 1 hour 5 minutes

2 cups all-purpose flour
1 teaspoon baking powder
¼ teaspoon salt
⅛ teaspoon **Ground Nutmeg**
1 cup (2 sticks) butter, softened
1¼ cups sugar
4 eggs
5 teaspoons **Pure Vanilla Extract**

1 MIX flour, baking powder, salt and Ground Nutmeg in small bowl; set aside.

2 BEAT butter and sugar in large bowl with electric mixer on medium speed 5 minutes or until light and fluffy. Beat in eggs one at a time. Stir in half of dry ingredients. Mix in Pure Vanilla Extract, then remaining dry ingredients. Pour batter into greased and floured 9x5x3-inch loaf pan.

3 BAKE in preheated 325°F oven 1 hour to 1 hour 5 minutes or until toothpick inserted in center comes out clean. Cool in pan on wire rack.

➤ **MAKES 12 SERVINGS**

flavor variations

● **VANILLA-ORANGE POUND CAKE**
Substitute 1 teaspoon **Orange Extract** for Pure Vanilla Extract. Stir 1 tablespoon grated orange zest into batter with dry ingredients. Prepare as directed.

● **GRILLED VANILLA POUND CAKE**
Prepare as directed. When completely cool, slice loaf into ½-inch-thick slices. Brush both sides of each slice with melted butter. Grill over direct medium heat about 1 minute on each side or until cake is marked and warm.

Mexican Spiced Pepita Brownies

PREP TIME: 10 minutes · COOK TIME: According to package directions, usually about 30 minutes

1 package (19½ ounces) fudge brownie mix
2 teaspoons instant coffee powder
1 teaspoon **Pure Vanilla Extract**
1 teaspoon **Ground Cinnamon**
¾ cup toasted pumpkin seeds, divided

1 **PREPARE** brownie mix according to package directions. Mix in instant coffee, Pure Vanilla Extract and Ground Cinnamon. Stir in ½ cup pumpkin seeds. Spread batter evenly in 8x8-inch baking pan. Sprinkle remaining ¼ cup pumpkin seeds over batter.

2 **BAKE** according to package directions. Let cool slightly before cutting.

▶ **MAKES 9 (2½-INCH) BROWNIES**

flavor variations

● SPICED PEANUT BROWNIES
Use ¾ cup toasted peanuts for the pumpkin seeds.

● SPICED ORANGE-PEPITA BROWNIES
Substitute ½ teaspoon **Orange Extract** for Pure Vanilla Extract.

Peppery Chocolate Chocolate-Chip Cookies

PREP TIME: 12 minutes, plus 30 minutes chilling time · COOK TIME: 10 minutes

1 package (12 ounces) mini semisweet
  chocolate chips, divided
2 cups all-purpose flour
1 teaspoon **Ground Black Pepper**
1 teaspoon baking soda
½ teaspoon salt
1 cup unsalted butter, at room temperature
⅔ cup light brown sugar
2 large eggs
1 teaspoon **Pure Vanilla Extract**

1 **MELT** 1¼ cups chocolate chips in microwave at 50% power, stopping at 1-minute intervals to stir. Set aside to cool. Sift flour, Ground Black Pepper, baking soda and salt together and set aside.

2 **BEAT** butter and sugar with electric mixer on medium speed until light and fluffy, 2 minutes. Beat in eggs one at a time. Add Pure Vanilla Extract. Stir in flour mixture. Fold in cooled chocolate and stir in remaining chocolate chips. Drop dough by tablespoonfuls onto nonstick cookie sheet, leaving about 1 inch between each cookie.

3 **BAKE** in preheated 350°F oven 10 to 12 minutes or until edges and tops are set. Remove from oven and transfer to wire rack to cool.

► MAKES ABOUT 2 DOZEN

flavor variations

● **PEPPERY CHOCOLATE CHOCOLATE-CHIP COOKIES 2**
Substitute 1 teaspoon **Coarse Ground Black Pepper** for **Ground Black Pepper**. Prepare as directed.

● **PEPPERY CINNAMON-CHOCOLATE COOKIES**
Add ½ teaspoon **Ground Cinnamon** to dry ingredients. Prepare as directed.

● **PEPPERY CHOCOLATE COOKIE ICE-CREAM SANDWICHES**
Prepare as directed. Use an ice cream scoop to scoop dough onto baking sheets, spacing scoops 2 inches apart. Flatten scoops slightly with fingers. Bake 12 to 14 minutes or until set. Let cookies cool completely, then scoop ¼ cup softened vanilla ice cream onto flat sides of half of cooled cookies. Top with remaining cookies and freeze until ice cream is set.

Cherry-Vanilla Clafoutis

PREP TIME: 15 minutes · COOK TIME: 25 minutes

3 large eggs, at room temperature
½ cup sugar
1 cup heavy cream
½ teaspoon **Pure Vanilla Extract**
½ cup all-purpose flour, sifted
¼ teaspoon **Ground Nutmeg**
⅛ teaspoon salt
1 pound sweet cherries, pitted
Confectioners' sugar for dusting

1 **WHISK** eggs and sugar in medium bowl until combined. Whisk in cream and Pure Vanilla Extract, then whisk in flour, Ground Nutmeg and salt.

2 **DIVIDE** batter evenly among 4 lightly greased 5-inch baking dishes. Sprinkle each with one-fourth of cherries.

3 **BAKE** in preheated 400°F oven 20 to 25 minutes or until set. Remove from oven, dust with confectioners' sugar, and serve warm.

► **MAKES FOUR 5-INCH CLAFOUTIS**

flavor variations

● **CHERRY-ALMOND CLAFOUTIS**
Substitute ¼ teaspoon **Almond Extract** for Pure Vanilla Extract. Prepare as directed.

● **BLUEBERRY-VANILLA CLAFOUTIS**
Use 2 cups fresh blueberries in place of cherries. Prepare as directed.

Spiced Summer Melon

PREP TIME: 5 minutes

1 ripe melon, such as honeydew or
  cantaloupe
1 teaspoon **Pumpkin Pie Spice**
1 teaspoon fresh lemon juice

1 **PEEL** and seed melon. Cut into cubes and transfer to medium bowl.

2 **SPRINKLE** melon with Pumpkin Pie Spice and toss to coat. Drizzle with lemon juice, toss again and serve.

► **MAKES 4 SERVINGS**

flavor variations

● **WATERMELON WITH LEMON AND CHILI**
Use 1 pound diced seedless watermelon
in place of cantaloupe or honeydew.
Substitute 1 teaspoon **Chili Powder** for
Pumpkin Pie Spice. Prepare as directed.

● **MELON WITH LIME AND RED PEPPER**
Substitute ½ teaspoon **Ground Red Pepper**
mixed with 1 teaspoon sugar for **Pumpkin
Pie Spice.** Use 1 teaspoon lime juice in
place of lemon juice. Prepare as directed.

Balsamic Strawberries with Black Pepper

PREP TIME: 15 minutes

¼ cup light brown sugar
1 tablespoon aged balsamic vinegar
2 pints strawberries, washed, stemmed and
   cut in half lengthwise
1 teaspoon **Coarse Ground Black Pepper**

Long-stemmed strawberries, for garnish
   (optional)

1 **STIR** sugar and vinegar in medium bowl until combined. Add strawberries and toss until coated. Let stand 5 minutes.

2 **DIVIDE** strawberry mixture evenly among four dessert dishes. Sprinkle each serving with ¼ teaspoon Coarse Ground Black Pepper. Garnish each serving with a long-stemmed strawberry, if desired.

► **MAKES 4 SERVINGS**

flavor variations

● **BALSAMIC STRAWBERRIES
WITH FROZEN YOGURT**
Prepare as directed. Spoon each serving over a scoop of vanilla frozen yogurt.

● **BALSAMIC STRAWBERRIES
WITH ANGEL FOOD CAKE**
Prepare as directed. Spoon each serving over a slice of angel food cake.

● **BALSAMIC-VANILLA STRAWBERRIES**
Add ½ teaspoon **Pure Vanilla Extract** to vinegar mixture. Prepare as directed.

Make-Ahead Meals

Citrus-Herb Chicken

PREP TIME: 5 minutes · **COOK TIME:** 8 minutes

½ cup plus 1 tablespoon olive oil
½ cup orange juice
1 tablespoon **Parsley Flakes**
2 teaspoons **Onion Powder**
2 teaspoons **Garlic Powder**
2 teaspoons salt
1½ teaspoons **Ground Black Pepper**
18 boneless, skinless chicken breasts
   (about 5 pounds)

1 **MIX** ½ cup oil, orange juice, Parsley Flakes, Onion Powder, Garlic Powder, salt and Ground Black Pepper in small bowl. Place chicken in large resealable plastic bag. Add marinade and seal. Knead bag until chicken is coated with mixture.

2 **HEAT** remaining 1 tablespoon oil in large nonstick skillet over medium heat. Cook chicken, several pieces at a time, 6 to 8 minutes per side, until golden and cooked through.

3 **DIVIDE** chicken into portions. Use one to make the evening's meal, then freeze remaining chicken or use to prepare recipes on pages 150 to 151.

► **MAKES 5 POUNDS**

freezing directions

Divide remaining chicken breasts among 4 resealable plastic bags. Label, date and refrigerate up to 3 days or freeze up to 3 months.

Chicken Quesadillas

PREP TIME: 10 minutes · COOK TIME: 5 minutes

8 (8-inch) flour tortillas
2 pieces Citrus-Herb Chicken, shredded
1 cup shredded Monterey Jack cheese
1½ teaspoons **Grill Mates® Montreal Chicken Seasoning**
2 tablespoons bottled green salsa, plus more for serving, if desired
4 teaspoons chopped scallions

1 **PLACE** 4 tortillas in single layer on baking sheet. Combine chicken, cheese and Chicken Seasoning in medium bowl. Divide mixture among tortillas. Top each with 2 teaspoons salsa and 1 teaspoon scallions. Top with remaining tortillas, pressing down around edges to seal.

2 **BAKE** in preheated 350°F oven 5 minutes or until cheese has melted and filling is hot. Cut into quarters and serve with additional salsa for dipping, if desired.

► MAKES 4 SERVINGS

Baked Chicken Parmigiana

PREP TIME: 10 minutes · COOK TIME: 20 minutes

3 cups 30-Minute Marinara (page 156)
4 pieces Citrus-Herb Chicken
1 cup shredded Mozzarella cheese
1 teaspoon **Basil Leaves**

> freezing directions
>
> Wrap tightly in plastic wrap, then aluminum foil. Label, date and freeze for up to 1 month. Unwrap and bake in preheated 350°F oven 45 minutes until heated through and sauce is bubbling.

1 **SPREAD** 1 cup Marinara in bottom of 8-inch baking pan. Top with chicken. Cover with 2 remaining cups marinara sauce. Toss Mozzarella cheese with Basil Leaves and sprinkle over chicken.

2 **BAKE** in preheated 350°F oven 20 minutes or until cheese is melted and sauce is bubbling. Let stand 5 minutes before serving.

► MAKES 4 SERVINGS

Spicy Chicken Wrapped in Foil

PREP TIME: 5 minutes · **COOK TIME:** 15 minutes

1 package **Enchilada Sauce Mix**
1 tablespoon diced pickled jalapeños
½ teaspoon **Oregano Leaves**
4 pieces Citrus-Herb Chicken
½ cup shredded Mexican cheese blend
2 cups cooked rice

> **freezing directions**
>
> Place packs in a resealable plastic bag. Label, date and freeze up to 1 month. Bake at 350°F for 35 minutes or until very hot.

1 **PREPARE** Enchilada Sauce Mix according to package directions. Stir in jalapeños and Oregano Leaves. Tear 4 pieces of heavy-duty aluminum foil 14 inches wide.

2 **PLACE** ½ cup cooked rice and 1 piece chicken in center of each piece of foil. Top each with ½ cup sauce, then 2 tablespoons cheese. Wrap tightly to seal completely.

3 **BAKE** in preheated 400°F oven 15 minutes until cheese is melted and sauce is bubbling.

▶ **MAKES 4 SERVINGS**

Cobb Salad

PREP TIME: 12 minutes

2 cups chopped Citrus-Herb Chicken
  (4 pieces)
1 ripe avocado, peeled, pitted and diced
1 tablespoon **Salad Supreme® Seasoning**
1 bag (10 ounces) chopped romaine lettuce
4 hard-boiled eggs, peeled and chopped
2 medium tomatoes, chopped
4 slices cooked bacon, crumbled

Bottled blue cheese salad dressing, for
  serving

TOSS chicken, avocado and Salad Supreme Seasoning in medium bowl until combined. Divide lettuce evenly among 4 salad bowls. Top each with heaping ½ cup chicken mixture. Sprinkle with hard-boiled eggs, then tomatoes. Top with crumbled bacon. Serve with dressing on the side.

▶ **MAKES 4 SERVINGS**

Seasoned Ground Beef

PREP TIME: 5 minutes · COOK TIME: 15 minutes

5 pounds ground beef
1 large onion, peeled and minced
1 tablespoon **Garlic Powder**
1½ teaspoons **Celery Salt**
1 teaspoon **Ground Black Pepper**
1 teaspoon salt

1 **MIX** all ingredients in large bowl. Spread beef mixture on nonstick rimmed baking sheet.

2 **BAKE** in preheated 350°F oven 5 minutes. Break mixture into marble size pieces. Continue cooking 5 to 10 minutes or until meat is completely browned.

3 **DIVIDE** cooked beef mixture into five 1-pound portions. Use one to make the evening's meal, then freeze remaining beef mixture or use to prepare recipes on pages 154 to 155.

► **MAKES 5 POUNDS**

freezing directions

Divide remaining beef among 4 resealable plastic bags. Label, date and refrigerate up to 3 days or freeze up to 3 months.

Tamale Pie

PREP TIME: 10 minutes · COOK TIME: 25 minutes

1 pound cooked Seasoned Ground Beef
1 package **Taco Seasoning Mix**
2 cans (10 ounces <u>each</u>) diced tomatoes
  with green chiles
1 cup thawed frozen corn kernels
1 cup instant grits, cooked according to
  package directions
1 cup shredded Cheddar cheese

freezing directions

Cover with heavy-duty aluminum foil. Label,
date and freeze up to 3 months. Bake covered
in preheated 375°F oven 15 minutes. Uncover
and bake 30 minutes or until heated through.

1 **HEAT** beef, Taco Seasoning Mix, tomatoes, and corn in medium saucepan over medium heat. Bring to a boil, cover and cook, stirring frequently, 5 minutes. Remove from heat. Spread mixture in 2-quart casserole. Stir together cheese and grits and spread over meat mixture.

2 **BAKE** in preheated 375°F oven 15 minutes or until very hot. Let stand 5 minutes before serving.

► **MAKES 6 SERVINGS**

Pizza-Pasta Casserole

PREP TIME: 10 minutes · COOK TIME: 30 minutes

1 tablespoon olive oil
½ cup diced green bell peppers
1 pound cooked Seasoned Ground Beef
8 ounces macaroni, cooked and drained
3½ cups marinara sauce
½ cup diced button mushrooms
½ teaspoon salt
½ teaspoon **Ground Black Pepper**
1 cup shredded Mozzarella cheese

freezing directions

Cover with heavy-duty aluminum foil. Label,
date and freeze up to 3 months. Bake covered
in preheated 350°F oven 15 minutes. Remove
foil and bake 30 minutes or until sauce is
bubbling and cheese is lightly colored.

1 **HEAT** oil in nonstick skillet over medium heat. Add bell peppers and sauté for 5 minutes. Combine beef, macaroni, marinara sauce, bell peppers and mushrooms in 2½-quart casserole dish, tossing to mix. Season with salt and Ground Black Pepper.

2 **BAKE** in preheated 350°F oven 20 minutes. Sprinkle with cheese and bake 10 minutes or until cheese has melted and browned slightly.

► **MAKES 6 SERVINGS**

 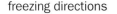

Sloppy Joe

PREP TIME: 5 minutes · COOK TIME: 10 minutes

1 pound cooked Seasoned Ground Beef
1 package **Sloppy Joe Seasoning Mix**
1 cup water
½ cup barbecue sauce
½ teaspoon **Ground Mustard**

6 rolls, split, for serving

1 **MIX** beef, Sloppy Joe Seasoning Mix, water, barbecue sauce and Ground Mustard in large skillet.

2 **HEAT** over medium-high heat. Bring to a boil. Reduce heat to low; cover and simmer 5 to 8 minutes, stirring occasionally, until sauce has thickened. Serve on rolls.

▶ **MAKES 6 SERVINGS**

Calzone

PREP TIME: 10 minutes · COOK TIME: 20 minutes

1 pound cooked Seasoned Ground Beef
1 cup shredded Mozzarella cheese
½ cup ricotta cheese
1 large egg
1 cup 30-Minute Marinara (page 156)
1 package (13 ounces) refrigerated pizza dough

1 **MIX** beef and cheeses in medium bowl. Stir in egg and Marinara. Set aside.

2 **DIVIDE** dough into 4 equal pieces. Roll out each piece on lightly floured surface to 7-inch round. Spoon an equal portion of beef mixture on each round, leaving 1-inch border. Fold dough over to make a semicircle. Pinch edges together and fold over to seal tightly. Place on nonstick baking sheet.

3 **BAKE** in preheated 425°F oven 20 minutes or until slightly puffed and golden brown.

▶ **MAKES 4 SERVINGS**

freezing directions

Wrap calzones individually in plastic wrap, then foil. Unwrap and bake in preheated 425°F oven 40 minutes or until golden and heated through.

30-Minute Marinara

PREP TIME: 10 minutes · COOK TIME: 20 minutes

¼ cup olive oil
1½ tablespoons **California Style® Wet Garlic**
3 cans (28 ounces <u>each</u>) crushed tomatoes
1 tablespoon **Basil Leaves**
1 tablespoon **Oregano Leaves**
½ teaspoon **Crushed Red Pepper**
1 tablespoon sugar
2 teaspoons salt
1 teaspoon **Ground Black Pepper**

1 **HEAT** olive oil in large pot or Dutch oven over medium heat. Add Wet Garlic and sauté 2 minutes. Add tomatoes, Basil Leaves, Oregano Leaves and Crushed Red Pepper. Bring to a simmer. Add sugar, salt and Ground Black Pepper.

2 **SIMMER** 15 minutes or until flavors have blended. (The sauce should remain vibrant red. If it is cooked too long, color will deepen and the tomatoes will become more acidic.)

3 **DIVIDE** cooked sauce into five 1-quart portions. Use one to make the evening's meal, then freeze remaining sauce or use to prepare recipes on pages 158 to 159.

► **MAKES ABOUT 5 QUARTS**

---

freezing directions

Divide sauce among 1-quart freezer containers. Cover, label and date. Freeze up to 3 months.

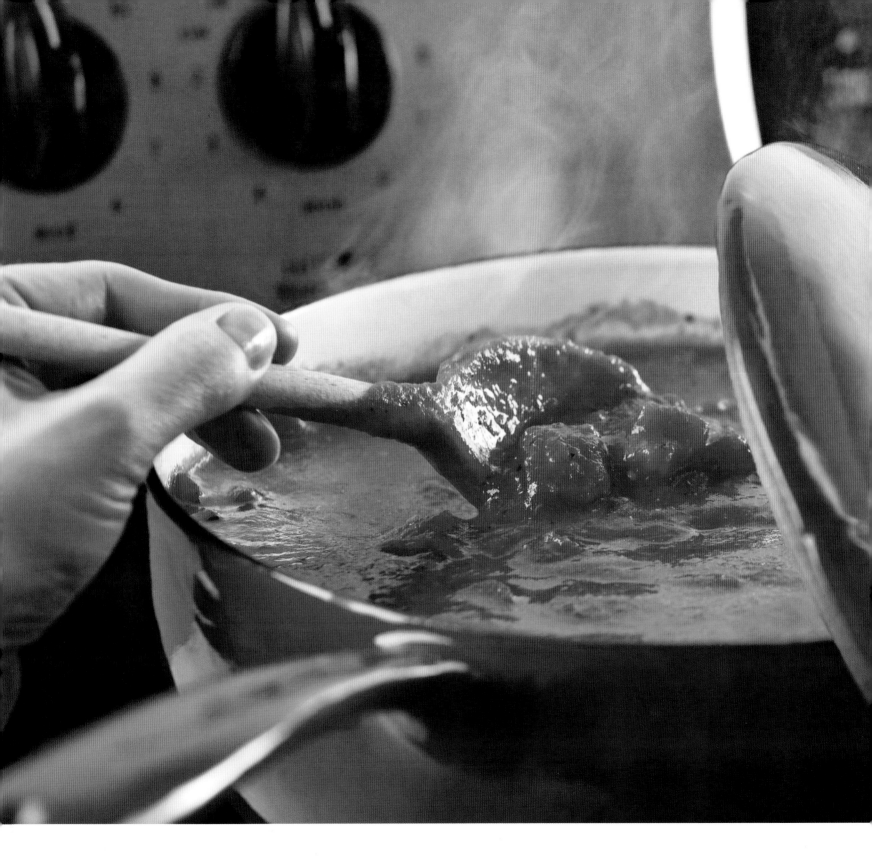

Cheese Lasagna

PREP TIME: 15 minutes · COOK TIME: 45 minutes

2 containers (15 ounces <u>each</u>) ricotta
  cheese
1 teaspoon **Italian Seasoning**
1 teaspoon **Parsley Flakes**
½ teaspoon salt
½ teaspoon **Ground Black Pepper**
4 cups 30-Minute Marinara
9 no-cook lasagna noodles
2½ cups shredded Mozzarella cheese
¼ cup grated Parmesan cheese

freezing directions

Wrap in plastic, then second layer of foil. Label,
date and freeze up to 3 months. Remove outer
foil and plastic before baking. Bake covered in
preheated 350°F oven 1 hour 15 minutes.
Uncover and bake 20 minutes until sauce is
bubbling and cheese is lightly colored. Let rest
15 minutes before cutting.

1 **MIX** ricotta, Italian Seasoning, Parsley Flakes, salt and Ground Black Pepper in medium bowl until blended. Spoon 1½ cups Marinara in the bottom of a 9x13-inch baking dish. Top with 3 noodles, then 2 cups ricotta; sprinkle with 1 cup Mozzarella. Top with ¾ cup Marinara, a layer of noodles, remaining ricotta, and 1 cup Mozzarella. Cover with ¾ cup Marinara and a final layer of noodles. Spoon the remaining 1 cup sauce over the noodles to cover. Sprinkle with the remaining ½ cup Mozzarella and Parmesan. Cover entire pan with heavy-duty aluminum foil. Can be refrigerated up to 24 hours.

2 **BAKE** in preheated 350°F oven 45 minutes. Remove foil and bake 20 minutes or until sauce is bubbling and cheese is lightly colored. Remove from oven and let stand 15 minutes before cutting.

► MAKES 12 SERVINGS

Spaghetti with Meat Sauce

PREP TIME: 5 minutes · COOK TIME: 15 minutes

1½ pounds dry spaghetti
1 pound cooked Seasoned Ground Beef
  (page 152)
5 cups 30-Minute Marinara

1 **COOK** spaghetti according to package directions.

2 **COMBINE** beef and Marinara in a saucepan over medium heat. Cook, stirring, 10 to 15 minutes or until slighly thickened and heated through.

► MAKES 6 SERVINGS

freezing directions

Divide sauce among 1-quart freezer containers.
Label, date and freeze up to 3 months.

Stuffed Shells

PREP TIME: 15 minutes · COOK TIME: 30 minutes if just made; 40 minutes if refrigerated

1 container (15 ounces) ricotta cheese
1¼ cup grated Parmesan cheese, divided
1 large egg
2 teaspoons **Parsley Flakes**
1 teaspoon **Basil Leaves**
½ teaspoon **Oregano Leaves**
¼ teaspoon **Garlic Powder**
¼ teaspoon **Onion Powder**
½ teaspoon salt
1½ cups shredded Mozzarella cheese
3 cups 30-Minute Marinara
12 jumbo pasta shells, cooked according to
   package directions for al dente, drained
   and cooled

freezing directions

Cover with heavy-duty aluminum foil. Label,
date and freeze up to 3 months. Bake covered
in preheated 350°F oven 15 minutes. Remove
the foil and bake 30 minutes or until the sauce
is bubbling and the cheese is lightly colored.

1 **MIX** ricotta, 1 cup Parmesan, egg, Parsley Flakes, Basil Leaves, Oregano Leaves, Garlic Powder, Onion Powder and salt. Set aside. Cover bottom of 2½-quart baking dish with 1½ cups Marinara. Fill each shell with 2 heaping tablespoons ricotta mixture. Arrange the stuffed shells in the Marinara. Cover with remaining Marinara.

2 **COMBINE** Mozzarella with remaining ½ cup Parmesan. Sprinkle over shells.

3 **BAKE** in preheated 350°F oven 20 minutes or until Marinara is bubbling and cheese is lightly colored.

▶ **MAKES 6 SERVINGS**

Vegetable Pizza

PREP TIME: 10 minutes · COOK TIME: 10 minutes

1 (12-inch) prepared pizza crust
½ cup 30-Minute Marinara
1 cup thinly sliced vegetables, such as
   button mushrooms, roasted red bell
   peppers, onions or zucchini
1 teaspoon **Basil Leaves**
1 cup shredded Mozzarella cheese
⅓ cup grated Parmesan cheese

1 **PLACE** crust on pizza stone or baking sheet. Spread Marinara evenly over crust. Top with vegetables and Basil Leaves. Sprinkle with Mozzarella and Parmesan.

2 **BAKE** in preheated 450°F oven 10 minutes or until cheese is bubbling and vegetables are cooked. Let stand 5 minutes before cutting.

▶ **MAKES 6 SERVINGS**

The Enspicelopedia™

Almond Extract

DESCRIPTION
Almond Extract is a flavoring produced by combining bitter-almond oil with ethyl alcohol. The almonds are heated, then the oils are extracted and combined with alcohol.

FLAVOR & AROMA PROFILE
Almond Extract has a strong nutty fragrance and a sweet almond flavor. The flavor is very intense, so it should be used sparingly.

USES
Pure almond flavoring is a baker's must. Because it is clear, it will not add any color and can be used to lend a delightfully nutty flavor to confections and baked goods.

ORIGINS & FOLKLORE
Almonds were among the earliest cultivated foods; there is evidence that they were grown before 3000 B.C.

When Arab traders settled in Portugal and Spain, they imported citrus and almond trees from their homelands. Eventually, almonds became a common part of the cuisine in Spain and Portugal.

In the 1700s, Franciscan monks brought almond trees from Spain to California and today, the San Joaquin and Sacramento Valleys are the chief almond-growing centers in the United States.

In classical times, Romans gave gifts of sugared almonds to important dignitaries as well as personal friends. At weddings, guests tossed almonds at the bride and groom as a symbol of fertility.

Basil

DESCRIPTION
Basil is a member of the mint family. Its botanical name is derived from the Greek "to be fragrant."

FLAVOR & AROMA PROFILE
Basil has a fresh, clean fragrance with green, minty flavor notes.

The Difference Between Spices and Herbs

Often, the word *spice* is used as a general term for all dried flavorings. But herbs and spices are two very different things.

SPICES are the dried bark, seeds or roots of plants. They are usually sold ground, but many of them can be found in their whole forms as well.

HERBS are the leafy green parts of a plant; they are available both fresh and dried. When they are sold dried, they are usually chopped (like basil) or rubbed (such as sage).

Dried herbs tend to have more intense flavor than fresh. The quality is also more consistent year-round; the flavor and quality of fresh herbs tend to fluctuate throughout the year.

USES

Basil is used in many Mediterranean dishes. It is used in green Thai curry blend, bouquet garni and Italian seasonings.

ORIGINS & FOLKLORE

Basil is believed to have originated in India, where it still grows wild.

In ancient Egypt, Basil was used in the embalming and mummification process. Through the centuries, it became a custom of young Italian suitors to wear a sprig of Basil as a sign of their marital intentions. In India, Hindus believed that if a leaf of Basil were buried with them, it would serve as their passport to heaven.

Bay Leaves

DESCRIPTION

Bay Leaves are the dried leaves of an evergreen tree.

FLAVOR & AROMA PROFILE

Bay Leaves' aromatic flavor is pungent and spicy, with cooling undertones and a pleasantly mild bitter aftertaste.

USES

Bay Leaves are an essential ingredient in warming winter meals, such as soups and stews. They are also used in Mediterranean, Indian, Middle Eastern and Caribbean cuisines.

ORIGINS & FOLKLORE

Bay Leaves are native to the Mediterranean area. Bay Leaves grown in Turkey are considered the finest in the world.

Champions of the Olympic games in ancient Greece wore garlands of Bay Leaves. The word *baccalaureate* alludes to the bay wreaths worn by poets and scholars when they received academic honors in ancient Greece.

Keeping Dried Herbs and Spices Fresh

For the most flavor, keep spices and herbs only as long as their flavor lasts.

Ground spices	2 to 3 years
Whole spices	3 to 4 years
Seasoning blends	1 to 2 years
Herbs	1 to 3 years
Extracts*	4 years

Here are some tips for keeping your spices fresh as long as possible (and for finding out if it is time to replace them):

● CHECK THE COLOR of spices and herbs. If it has faded, chances are the flavor has too.

● RUB OR CRUSH the spice or herb in your hand. If the aroma is weak, it's time to replace it.

● STORE herbs and spices in tightly capped containers and keep them away from heat, moisture and direct sunlight.

● TO MINIMIZE MOISTURE and caking, use a dry measuring spoon and avoid sprinkling directly from the jar into a steaming pot. Replace lids immediately after use and make sure they are tightly closed.

● CHECK THE FRESHNESS DATE on the bottom or right side of the bottle to help keep track of when it's time to toss (visit mccormick.com for more information).

* (except Pure Vanilla Extract, which lasts indefinitely)

Black Pepper

FLAVOR & AROMA PROFILE
Black Pepper has a sharp, penetrating aroma and a characteristic woody, piney flavor.

USES
Black Pepper adds flavor to almost every food of every nation in the world. It is used in rubs, spice blends, salad dressings and peppercorn blends.

ORIGINS & FOLKLORE
Black Pepper is considered the "king of the spices" by many spice buyers due to its popularity and historical significance. Pepper was so precious in ancient times that it was used as money to pay taxes, tributes, dowries and rent. In 410 A.D., when Rome was captured, 3,000 pounds of pepper were demanded as ransom.

DESCRIPTION
Black Peppercorns are the dried berries of a vine. The berries are picked while still green, allowed to ferment and are then sun-dried until they shrivel and turn a brownish-black color.

Chili Powder

DESCRIPTION
Chili Powder is a combination of ground chiles, cumin, oregano, garlic and salt.

FLAVOR & AROMA PROFILE
Chili Powder lends smoky and spicy flavor to all kinds of dishes.

USES
Chili Powder is the essential flavoring ingredient in chili. It can also be used to add Southwestern flavor to bean dishes, guacamole and baked goods.

• •

Cinnamon

DESCRIPTION
Cinnamon is the dried inner bark of various species of evergreen trees. At harvest, the bark is stripped off and put in the sun, where it curls into the quill shape that we know as Cinnamon Sticks.

FLAVOR & AROMA PROFILE
Cinnamon is characteristically woody, musty and earthy in flavor and aroma.

USES
Cinnamon is popular in sweet baked dishes, with fruits and in confections. Cinnamon is also widely used in savory dishes around the world such as moles, curries, tagines and barbecue.

ORIGINS & FOLKLORE
Cinnamon imported from Indonesia is the most common form sold in the United States. It has a milder red-hot flavor followed by a pleasantly woody note. Vietnam is the source for Saigon Cinnamon, which is considered the finest variety available and has a bold spicy-sweet flavor.

The word cinnamon means "sweet wood" in Malay. The ancient Romans believed Cinnamon to be sacred and burned it at funerals.

Cinnamon was one of the first spices sought in 15th-century European explorations, and some say it indirectly led to the discovery of America.

• •

Cumin

DESCRIPTION
Cumin is the dried seed of an herb that is a member of the parsley family.

FLAVOR & AROMA PROFILE
Cumin has a pungent earthy flavor.

USES
The flavor of Cumin plays a major role in Mexican, Thai, Vietnamese and Indian cuisines. Cumin is a critical ingredient of chili powder, and is found in adobos, garam masala and curry powder.

ORIGINS & FOLKLORE

Superstition during the Middle Ages cited that Cumin kept chickens and lovers from wandering. It was also believed that a happy life awaited the bride and groom who carried Cumin Seed throughout the wedding.

Dill

DESCRIPTION

Dill is a member of the parsley family and is related to anise, caraway, coriander, cumin and fennel. Dill Weed is the dried leaves of the same plant from which Dill Seed comes.

FLAVOR & AROMA PROFILE

Dill Weed has a more subtle, fresh flavor than the seeds. It is characterized by sweet, tea-like and rye notes; the seeds tend to be warmer in flavor.

USES

European and American cuisines use Dill Seed in pickles, meats, seafood, cheeses and breads. Dill Weed is also used with fish and shellfish.

ORIGINS & FOLKLORE

Dill's name comes from the Old Norse *dilla,* meaning "to lull," and was once given to crying babies. Dill is also thought to cure hiccups, stomachaches, insomnia and bad breath. The most famous use of Dill, the Dill pickle, is at least 400 years old.

Ginger

DESCRIPTION

Ginger is the underground stem of a plant that grows 2 to 3 feet tall.

FLAVOR & AROMA PROFILE

The flavor of Ginger is a unique combination of citrus, soapy and earthy flavor notes.

USES

Ginger is used in baked goods, curries and in spice blends around the world.

ORIGINS & FOLKLORE

Ginger's name is derived from a Sanskrit word meaning "horn-shaped" or "horn-root." During the 15th century, gingerbread became a gift of love and respect. In the 1800s, Ginger was commonly sprinkled on top of beer or ale, then stirred into the drink with a hot poker—thus the invention of ginger ale.

Intensify the Flavor of Seed Spices

Chefs have long prized whole seed spices for their fresh flavor and aroma, which are released at the moment the seed is ground or crushed. An easy way to intensify the flavor of seed spices is to toast them before using them in a recipe.

1. Heat a dry skillet over medium heat.
2. Once skillet is hot, pour in desired amount of seeds.
3. Using a spatula, stir the seeds in the pan until they become fragrant, approximately 1 to 2 minutes.

Lemon Extract

DESCRIPTION
Lemon Extract is made by pressing the outer peel, which contains the lemon oil, and combining the oil with ethyl alcohol.

FLAVOR & AROMA PROFILE
Lemon Extract has a strong, clear lemon aroma and true lemon flavor.

USES
Mostly used in baking (especially cheesecakes and often mixed with lemon zest) or added to fish and poultry marinades. Also used in glazes, frostings and candy-making.

ORIGINS & FOLKLORE
Lemons were once used by the British Royal Navy to combat scurvy, a disease caused by a deficiency of vitamin C.

Nutmeg

DESCRIPTION
Nutmeg is the seed of the same fruit from which mace is derived.

FLAVOR & AROMA PROFILE
Nutmeg's oval-shaped seeds have a sweet, spicy flavor.

USES
Nutmeg enhances both sweet and savory foods. Nutmeg blends well with other spices and is found in cuisines around the globe including those of Italy, the Caribbean, France, India, Germany, Scandinavia, Greece, Latin America and the Middle East.

ORIGINS & FOLKLORE
In colonial times, peddlers sold whittled wooden "nutmegs" to unsuspecting housewives.

Paprika

DESCRIPTION
Paprika is the dried, ground pods of a sweet red pepper. It is prized for its brilliant color.

FLAVOR & AROMA PROFILE
Most Paprika is mild and slightly sweet in flavor with a pleasantly fragrant aroma. Unlike regular Spanish Paprika, which is well known for the visual appearance it gives to dishes, Smoked Paprika is known for its smoky-sweet flavor profile. Derived from naturally smoked sweet red peppers, this Smoked Paprika provides a fantastic smoked flavor and brilliant red color to items such as chicken, beef, potatoes and rice.

USES
Paprika is used in seasoning blends and the cuisines of India, Morocco, Europe and the Middle East.

ORIGINS & FOLKLORE
Spanish explorers took red pepper seeds back to Europe, where the plant evolved into "sweet" Paprika. Pound for pound, Paprika has more vitamin C than citrus fruit.

Rosemary

DESCRIPTION
The slender, slightly curved leaves of Rosemary resemble miniature curved pine needles. Rosemary grows under harsh mountainous conditions.

FLAVOR & AROMA PROFILE
Rosemary has a distinctive pine-woody aroma with a fresh, bittersweet flavor.

USES
Rosemary is found in bouquet garni, herbes de Provence and seasoning blends for lamb and Mediterranean cuisines.

ORIGINS & FOLKLORE
In ancient Greece, Rosemary was valued for its alleged ability to strengthen the brain and memory. Also known as the "herb of remembrance," Rosemary was often placed on the graves of English heroes.

Saffron

DESCRIPTION
Saffron is the dried yellow stigmas of a flower in the Iris family. It takes 225,000 of them to make 1 pound of saffron.

FLAVOR & AROMA PROFILE
Saffron is used sparingly because its odor and flavor are so strong. The taste is spicy, pleasantly bitter and slightly honey-like.

USES
Saffron is used in spice blends for paella, curry, kheer and bouillabaisse.

ORIGINS & FOLKLORE
Spain is considered the premium source of Saffron.

Saffron is the most expensive spice in the world. The ancient Assyrians used saffron for medicinal purposes. The Greeks and Romans used it to perfume their luxurious baths. The bright orange-yellow color also made saffron useful as a dye.

Sage

DESCRIPTION
Sage leaves are silvery green in color.

Cut Sage refers to leaves that have been cut rather than ground into smaller pieces. **Rubbed Sage** is put through minimum grinding and a coarse sieve. The result is a fluffy, almost cotton-like product, unique among ground herbs. More Sage is sold in the rubbed form than any other.

FLAVOR & AROMA PROFILE
Sage is highly aromatic and is characterized by a medicinal, pine-woody flavor.

USES
Sage is used in Greek, Italian and other European cuisines. It is used to season sausages, poultry and fish.

ORIGINS & FOLKLORE
Historically, southeastern Europe has been the principal producer of Sage. Dalmatian Sage, as it is commonly called, has been recognized as superior in the United States. It is highly aromatic, noted for its mellowness. Its smoother taste is due to differing essential oil components.

Sage has been traditionally used for its antioxidant and antimicrobial properties. Sage was used during the Middle Ages to treat maladies such as fevers, liver disease and epilepsy. One common belief was that Sage strengthened the memory, hence a sage, or wise man, who always had a long memory. During the 1600s, the Chinese exchanged three to four pounds of their tea with Dutch traders for one pound of European Sage leaves.

Vanilla

Vanilla is derived from the dried, cured beans or fruit pods of a member of the Orchid family; this is the only orchid that produces edible fruit. Although Vanilla beans are sometimes used in their whole form, they are most commonly used for producing extracts and flavors.

Vanilla has a delicate, sweet and rich flavor and a spicy, recognizable fragrance.

Vanilla is used as a flavoring principally in sweet foods and also as a fragrantly tenacious ingredient in perfumery.

Vanilla was enjoyed by the Aztecs in a drink called *xoco-lall*, which was made from cocoa and Vanilla beans. The explorer Hernando Cortéz sampled this drink and returned to Spain with reports that it contained magical powers.

•

Grill Mates® Montreal Steak Seasoning

A bold blend of black pepper, garlic and select spices, Grill Mates® Montreal Steak Seasoning is known as "the flavor you can see." This chunky blend will make you the master of the grill and give you that special ingredient all your friends and family will ask for.

•

OLD BAY® Seasoning

OLD BAY Seasoning is a mixture of more than a dozen herbs and spices, including celery, bay leaves, mustard, red pepper and ginger. OLD BAY's flavor is pungent, earthy, citrusy and warming to taste.

OLD BAY Seasoning was created in 1939 by Gustav Brunn, a German immigrant with dreams of starting a spice business. Originally available only in the Chesapeake Bay area, OLD BAY's popularity has spread across the United States and Canada.

Once the preferred seasoning for crabs and shrimp, OLD BAY is now popular in non-seafood dishes as well. Hamburgers, fried chicken and gumbo are also flavored with OLD BAY.

Index